DINNER A.S.A.P.

150 Recipes Made *As Simple As Possible*

DINNER A.S.A.P.

150 Recipes Made *As Simple As Possible*

By the Editors of Cooking Light

Oxmoor House®

Published by Oxmoor House, an imprint of Time Inc. Books
225 Liberty Street, 4th Floor, New York, NY 10281

Writer: Danny S. Bonvissuto
Senior Editor: Rachel Quinlivan West, R.D.
Editor: Sarah A. Gleim
Assistant Project Editor: Melissa Brown
Art Director: Christopher Rhoads
Junior Designer: AnnaMaria Jacob
Executive Photography Director: Iain Bagwell
Photographers: Hélène Dujardin, Victor Protasio
Senior Photo Stylist: Kay E. Clarke
Photo Stylist: Amanda Widis
Food Stylists: Nathan Carrabba, Victoria E. Cox,
    Margaret Monroe Dickey, Catherine Crowell Steele
Test Kitchen Manager: Alyson Moreland Haynes
Senior Recipe Developer and Tester: Callie Nash
Recipe Developers and Testers: Julia Levy, Karen Rankin
Assistant Production Director: Sue Chodakiewicz
Senior Production Manager: Greg A. Amason
Copy Editors: Adrienne Davis, Kate Johnson
Proofreaders: Norma Butterworth-McKittrick,
    Jacqueline Giovanelli
Indexer: Nanette Cardon
Nutritional Analysis: Jessica Cox, R.D.N.
Fellows: Jessica Baude, Dree Deacon,
    Nicole Fisher, Rishon Hanners, Olivia Pierce,
    Natalie Schumann, Mallory Short

ISBN-13: 9-780-8487-4640-7
ISBN-10: 0-8487-4640-6
Library of Congress Control Number: 2015955932

Printed in the United States of America

10 9 8 7 6 5 4 3 2 1

First Printing 2016

CONTENTS

INTRODUCTION   6

DINNER A.S.A.P. 101   8

SEASONAL PRODUCE GUIDE   12

SUPERMARKET SUPPERS   16

EXPEDITED ENTRÉES   78

SUPERFAST SIDES   144

CHOP CHOP SALADS   186

10-MINUTE TREATS   230

EASY EXTRAS   264

NUTRITIONAL INFORMATION   282

METRIC EQUIVALENTS   283

INDEX   284

INTRODUCTION

When we set out to develop *Cooking Light Dinner A.S.A.P.*, the goal was to create a cookbook with simple, yet wholesome, recipes designed around the way today's busy, health-conscious cooks prepare dinner. You *can* create healthy—and delicious—meals in 25 minutes or less, and *Dinner A.S.A.P.* shows you how to do that, and more.

Our key strategy to the easy-to-follow recipes is utilizing premade and prechopped foods from your grocery store's deli, bakery, and frozen sections as starting points to help with menu prep. We even toss in simple tips throughout to help you shave off even more time for those nights you're really in a rush.

And because the right groceries are such critical elements to our recipes, we include a Dinner A.S.A.P. 101 guide to help you with your shopping and cooking strategies; a Seasonal Produce Guide so you can make healthy choices and swap out ingredients based on what fruits and vegetables are at their freshest; and a Get Equipped section with details on what kitchen tools you should always have on hand—so you can always make Dinner A.S.A.P.—as simple as possible.

Sarah Gleim, Editor

DINNER A.S.A.P. 101

Imagine a vine-ripened summer tomato sprinkled with salt. A big bowl of linguine tossed with olive oil, basil, and shaved Parmesan. A fresh pink fillet of salmon dotted with dill. That's cooking A.S.A.P.—as simple as possible.

As anyone who's spent hours in the kitchen creating food they didn't enjoy afterward knows, long, drawn-out techniques can make cooking feel like a chore. Far from boring, *Dinner A.S.A.P.* is a philosophy that brings seasonality, quality ingredients, and smart, simple methods to the plate.

WHAT'S FOR DINNER?

It's the million-dollar question you have to answer every single night—whether you're prepared to or not. The good news is finding that answer can be simple when you cook smart. Start by always keeping a few staple foods on hand. A ball of prepared pizza dough, a jar of sauce, and preshredded cheese equal pizza in a pinch. Frozen ground beef and a few buns can quickly become a backyard picnic. Boxed pasta, sliced garlic, olive oil, and a light sprinkle of Parmesan cheese make a fast, filling meal. Bonus points for taking the extra three minutes to put a fried egg on top.

SHOPPING STRATEGIES

So how do you cook smart? Start by shopping smart. You may be alone in the kitchen, but grocery stores are full of sous chefs waiting to make your life easier. Instead of sawing your way through a pork shoulder at home, have the grocery store butcher trim and cube it for you. Fishmongers are happy to slice off skin, devein shrimp, and fillet fish. And precut veggies—especially butternut squash—are often worth the additional price to save on prep time. That's shopping the *Dinner A.S.A.P.* way. Utilize already prepared foods from your grocer's deli, salad bar, hot bar, and frozen section to save even more time and get dinner on the table A.S.A.P.—just make smart choices so you're not sacrificing your health to cut back prep time.

And don't be afraid to hit up a variety of specialty markets when you have time—you'll be surprised at the delicious items you can find that are great for pushing your pantry past its culinary comfort zone. These gourmet shops and ethnic groceries are full of sauces, spices, produce, and proteins that can quickly make an everyday meal go global. Something as simple as an Asian hot sauce or Indian cracker can drive a dish in a different direction.

COOKING SMART

Former President Dwight D. Eisenhower once said, "Plans are worthless, but planning is everything." Everything doesn't always go as planned in the kitchen, but visualizing the meal from start to finish can prevent missteps. Before you start, think about each part of the meal, the ingredients, and how they'll be prepared. Then consider how to coordinate each element—salad, entrée, sides—so they all arrive on the table together. And practice what chefs call *mise en place*, which means getting all ingredients and equipment together in one place to set yourself up for success.

Whenever possible, make two meals out of one. Making a batch of soup? Double the recipe, and freeze half for later. But you don't even have to work that hard: Serve braised pork shoulder with couscous and steamed broccoli one night, and then use the leftover pork in quesadillas, stuffed peppers, or potato hash a few nights later. That's *Dinner A.S.A.P.* And don't think the freezer is just for saving portions you couldn't eat—it's also a great place for extra ingredients to chill out until they're needed. Spoon extra tomato paste, chiles in adobo sauce, or even wine into ice-cube trays—just pop one out, thaw, and include in any recipe. (Look for Fast Freeze and Eat Now & Later tips throughout the book.)

When time permits, set aside a few hours in your week (Sundays are good) to tackle meal prep for the week ahead. Chop fresh veggies for recipes; make healthy, grab-and-go snacks; and knock out elements that require extra time, such as roasted garlic, caramelized onions, and dried beans or chickpeas.

GET EQUIPPED

Never underestimate the power of cooking equipment. Get to know what's in your kitchen—and how to use it properly. For instance, a hot skillet gives fish, meat, and vegetables a restaurant-quality sear, while a slow cooker braises meats low and slow—it's important to know the difference.

Properly seared meats and veggies should be caramelized to intensify their flavor profiles. To get the best sear, use a stainless steel or cast-iron pan, a touch of oil, and high heat, and resist the urge to move the food or pan (you're not sautéing). Most foods will stick to the pan at first—especially meats—but will let go when the sear is just right.

The slow cooker, on the other hand, is like a personal chef who's at home cooking when you're not. Use it to braise meats for barbecue, cook chickpeas for homemade hummus, or make chili.

THE SPICE IS RIGHT

Finally, properly seasoned foods are delicious tasting foods. A chicken breast on its own? Not so exciting. But a chicken breast atop a nest of fresh pappardelle or rubbed with artisan olive oil and lemon-scented salt to crisp up its skin?

Now you're talking. Go all out and splurge on oils, seasonings, and vinegars in specialty stores—especially on items like truffle oil that have a long shelf life and are used sparingly. The smallest details can make a big difference.

And take this advice with a grain of salt: A little salt and freshly ground black pepper go a long way. Think of the incredible flavor a roasted chicken has with a few pinches of both. Keep a saltcellar full of kosher grains and a pepper mill within reach of your prep area, and taste and season as you cook.

Just remember, every part of the meal doesn't have to be wow-worthy. Pick one element to be the star, and let the rest act as the supporting cast.

SEASONAL PRODUCE GUIDE

Every great meal starts with fresh produce harvested in its peak season. Here's how to pick and prepare the freshest fruits and vegetables any time of the year.

SPRING

APRICOTS: In season from May to August, apricots make a wonderful warm-weather snack. They're low in calories; full of beta-carotene, potassium, vitamin C, and fiber; and perfectly portable.

ARTICHOKES: Once you get past the pointy leaves—just snip the tips off with scissors—artichokes open up a world of possibilities. They're full of iron, potassium, magnesium, and vitamin C and best March through May. Pair them with dips, and let those leaves serve as tender, edible scoops.

ARUGULA: Also called rocket, arugula is known for its peppery taste. This member of the mustard family makes a lively addition to salads, works wonderfully in pesto, and serves as a bright topping for grilled pizzas.

ASPARAGUS: The greatest thing about these green spears is their versatility: They do beautifully on the grill, roasted with olive oil, and even shaved raw into salads. To keep them from drooping before dinner, submerge the ends in a shallow bowl of water to keep them fresh.

CARROTS: These colorful root veggies (usually orange, although purple, red, white, and yellow varieties are available) are at their peak in both spring and fall. They're full of beta-carotene and vitamin A, and a good source of vitamins B6 and K. Choose carrots that are crisp and free of blemishes, and store them in the coldest part of your refrigerator.

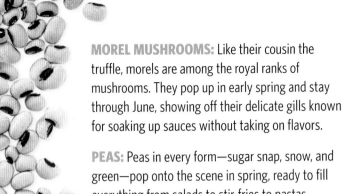

MOREL MUSHROOMS: Like their cousin the truffle, morels are among the royal ranks of mushrooms. They pop up in early spring and stay through June, showing off their delicate gills known for soaking up sauces without taking on flavors.

PEAS: Peas in every form—sugar snap, snow, and green—pop onto the scene in spring, ready to fill everything from salads to stir-fries to pastas.

RADISHES: Few veggies outside the pepper family pack heat like radishes. Look for ones with a deep color, solid roots, and green tops that give salads a subtle kick.

RHUBARB: Don't let those red stalks stump you: Rhubarb is a vegetable often treated like fruit. Though the greens aren't edible, the stalks become tart when paired with sugar and bring a bright color to everything from sauces to pies.

SPRING ONIONS: Also known as green onions or scallions, spring onions are baby onions picked before the bulb grows bigger. Avoid slimy leaves, and trim the roots and tops. Use them as a garnish, in omelets, or charred on the grill for smoky flavor.

STRAWBERRIES: No matter what the calendar says, it's officially spring when juicy red strawberries start showing up at the farmers' market. In peak season from April to June, they pack a nutritional punch: 1 cup supplies 100% of your daily vitamin C.

SWEET CHERRIES: Blink and you'll miss them: Sweet cherries are in their prime from late spring to early summer. Perfect for snacking or baking (Did someone say pie?), they're full of anthocyanins, which studies suggest may reduce risk for heart disease and cancer.

SUMMER

BASIL: A member of the mint family, basil enjoys its peak season in summer. Look for green leaves devoid of wilt or spots, and use this popular herb in sweet or savory applications.

BLUEBERRIES: Good for so much more than decorating that flag cake on the Fourth of July, blueberries are high in antioxidants that fight heart disease, cancers, and other health issues. They're best stored in a single layer away from moisture.

CORN: Technically a type of grass, corn is the darling of backyard barbecues from May to September. Look for a fresh husk with brown silk tips, and don't be afraid to peel it back and give those kernels a pinch to see if they're nice and milky.

EGGPLANT: Skin on or skin off, it's up to you, but we do love the purple hue eggplant adds to the dish. Store them on the counter, and work them into everything from crostini to grilled sandwiches.

FIGS: These low-maintenance fruits need little more than a rinse and stem trim before being paired with melon, cheeses, and cured meats. They keep best in the moist environment of the refrigerator produce drawer.

OKRA: Though it has a reputation for being gummy when overcooked, okra is an absolute delight fresh from the stalk. Each piece should have some give and not feel wooden or hard. Sauté them whole; slice, coat them with cornmeal, and pan fry; pickle them; or use them to flavor and thicken a big pot of gumbo.

PEACHES: Nothing says summer like a long bead of peach juice dripping down your chin. From May to September, Georgia's state fruit shines in jams and chutneys, in salads, in ice cream, and even on the grill.

PLUMS: Perfect off the vine and often used to sweeten sauces, the best plums fall just short of firm with a little give to the touch.

SUMMER SQUASH: Bigger isn't always better when it comes to squash: Pick small ones with bright-colored skin. Unlike their winter cousins, both the skins and seeds of summer squash are edible.

TOMATOES: In the thick of summer, when you can't even think of firing up the stove, a simple tomato sandwich or salad always does the trick. Keep the ripe ones at room temperature and out of the sunlight.

WATERMELON: It's tempting to scoop up a watermelon as soon as the weather gets warmer, but their season doesn't start until mid-June. Look for a dull rind devoid of bruises, and use the flesh in everything from margaritas to salsa.

ZUCCHINI: Full of vitamins A and C, fiber, and water, zucchini requires very little work to make it sing. Shave it raw into a salad, or use its ribbons in place of pasta with a fresh tomato sauce on top.

FALL

APPLES: Though they're available year-round, apples are at their peak from September to November. Use your eyes and hands to spot bruises and your nose to detect smells that indicate the fruit is past its prime.

BRUSSELS SPROUTS: The smallest members of the cabbage family grow on stalks and work well as an appetizer, side dish, or salad (pluck the leaves, blanch, dry, and toss with vinaigrette). Choose smaller heads for a sweeter taste.

CAULIFLOWER: This cabbage cousin is most notable for its white florets, but it also comes in purple, orange, and green varieties. Look for green leaves that haven't yellowed. Throw it into salads raw, or roast it up with other fall veggies.

FIGS: One of the few fruits that straddles two seasons, figs are ripe in early summer and again in late summer through the fall. Don't discard the shriveled ones—it's not an indication of age.

MUSHROOMS: Mushrooms are available all year long, but fall is their favorite season. Whenever possible, hand-select mushrooms to check for dark spots and damage on all sides.

PEARS: As versatile as the apple, pears fill fall tables with their sweet scent. Give the area near the stem a light push with your thumb—if you feel a little resistance, it's ripe.

PUMPKINS: Fall's favorite decoration looks just as good on the plate. Much better than canned, fresh pumpkin is well worth the extra effort. Look for tough-skinned gourds between 5 and 8 pounds.

QUINCE: One of the few fruits that's better when cooked, quince looks like the love child of an apple and a pear. When cooked, they have a grainy, pear-like texture. Look for them from October to December in farmers' markets.

SAGE: In a sea of green herbs, there's no mistaking sage, with its long, fuzzy leaves and distinctive woodsy smell. Refrigerate fresh leaves in a damp paper towel in a plastic bag.

SHALLOTS: Available year-round, shallots are smaller than onions and have less water, finer layers, and more concentrated flavor. Look for firmness and heft, and store them in a cool, dry place.

SWEET POTATOES: There's a big difference between pale- and dark-skinned sweet potatoes. The pale variety has a light yellow flesh and a crumbly texture when cooked. It's not as sweet as its darker counterpart, which has thick, dark orange skin and bright orange flesh.

WINTER SQUASH: Winter squash are picked in the fall and last until spring. Look for full, corky stems, and work those acorn, spaghetti, and butternut beauties into everything from chilis to gratins.

WINTER

BEETS: The best beets are small with stems and leaves intact. Use their bright colors—reds, yellows, and purples—to add life and flavor to winter meals.

BLOOD ORANGES: Work citrus into the winter with blood oranges in salads, salsas, and jams. Popular varieties include Moro and Tarocco; give them a grab, and discard those that feel spongy.

BROCCOLI RABE: Also known as rapini, the greens, buds, and stems of this winter plant are edible. It's a bitter green packed with vitamin K that works well in place of spinach.

CRANBERRIES: Raw cranberries make for bright holiday décor but have to be cooked to release their sweet flavor. Look for bright berries, and use them to flavor cakes, stews, jams, and that traditional Thanksgiving turkey.

KALE: This winter green gets lots of love for its incredible health benefits—fiber; folate; omega-3s; and vitamins A, C, and K. Look for fresh bunches of unwilted leaves; refrigerate in a plastic bag with a paper towel.

KUMQUATS: Best from December through April, kumquats are the only member of the citrus family with an edible peel. They closely resemble an orange but are much smaller.

LEEKS: Milder than green onions, leeks are better cooked than raw. Give them a good wash—dirt likes to creep up through the layers—and use them to flavor soups and stocks.

LEMONS: Whether you're adding acidity to a dish or showing off its bright yellow color, lemons create balance. Leave the green ones to ripen a little longer.

ORANGES: Juice, zest, or section and serve—oranges have endless applications. And they're one of a few fruits for which brown patches don't indicate damage.

PARSNIPS: This cream-colored root vegetable is similar to the carrot and is high in vitamins and minerals, especially antioxidants. Look for small or medium parsnips that are firm throughout.

POMEGRANATES: The inedible shell of the pomegranate is like a jewel box that holds tiny treasures of seeds and pulp. Look for heavy, bright orbs, and don't hesitate to ask for a sample.

TURNIPS: In winter, turnip greens become sweet and make a vitamin-packed side dish. Boil, mash, or puree the roots as an alternative to potatoes.

CHAPTER 1
SUPERMARKET SUPPERS

Think of the grocery store as your personal prep kitchen—an aisle-by-aisle pantry filled with ready-made foods that double the deliciousness and chop your effort in half. Peeled and deveined shrimp from the fish counter. Peanut-crusted chicken cutlets from the deli. Cooked brown rice from the freezer section. Using those shortcut ingredients and these recipes will make your healthy, complete dinners come together A.S.A.P.—as simple as possible.

CHICKEN MEATBALL ANGEL HAIR PASTA

Preformed, gluten-free meatballs simmer in marinara while angel hair pasta boils to perfection. No time to make spinach salad? Hit up your grocer's salad bar instead.

SERVES 6 • HANDS-ON TIME: 10 MIN. • TOTAL TIME: 20 MIN.

2 cups lower-sodium marinara sauce (such as Dell' Amore)

1 (12-ounce) package refrigerated spinach-and-garlic chicken meatballs, quartered (such as Bilinski's)

12 ounces uncooked angel hair pasta

2 tablespoons olive oil

1½ tablespoons red wine vinegar

½ teaspoon honey

¼ teaspoon Dijon mustard

⅛ teaspoon freshly ground black pepper

1 (6-ounce) package fresh baby spinach

¾ cup grilled red onion, coarsely chopped

2 ounces crumbled feta cheese (about ½ cup)

Basil leaves (optional)

1 Combine marinara sauce and meatball pieces in a medium saucepan. Bring to a boil; cover, reduce heat, and simmer 10 minutes or until thoroughly heated.

2 While sauce simmers, cook pasta according to package directions. Drain.

3 Combine olive oil and next 4 ingredients (through pepper) in a large bowl, stirring with a whisk. Add spinach, grilled onion, and feta cheese. Toss gently until spinach is coated.

4 Place pasta on each of 6 plates; spoon meatball sauce evenly over pasta. Sprinkle with basil leaves, if desired. Serve with spinach salad.

SERVING SIZE: about 1 cup pasta, ⅔ cup meatball sauce, and about 1 cup salad

CALORIES 429; FAT 13.5g (sat 3.3g, mono 5.1g, poly 1.5g); PROTEIN 19g; CARB 54g; FIBER 5g; SUGARS 7g (est. added sugars 4g); CHOL 53mg; IRON 4mg; SODIUM 811mg; CALC 126mg

Eat Now & Later

Line a crusty baguette or sourdough roll with the meatballs, layer with sauce, leftover grilled onion, and feta. Heat and eat!

CHICKEN AND BLACK BEAN TOSTADAS
WITH CILANTRO SLAW

Tacos, burritos, and quesadillas get lots of love, but tostadas are the easiest of all the Mexican meals. If you can't find the Southwestern-style grilled chicken breast strips in the produce or deli section, simply substitute rotisserie chicken.

SERVES 4 • HANDS-ON TIME: 15 MIN. • TOTAL TIME: 15 MIN.

1   (8-ounce) package refrigerated natural Southwestern-style grilled chicken breast strips, coarsely chopped (1¾ cups; such as Applegate Farms)
1   tablespoon canola oil
1   tablespoon fresh lime juice
⅛   teaspoon salt
2   cups bagged angel hair slaw
⅓   cup thinly sliced green onions (about 3 small)
¼   cup chopped fresh cilantro
4   (0.63-ounce) commercial tostada shells (such as Guerrero)
1   cup canned refried black beans (such as Bush's Cocina Latina Frijoles Negros Machacados)
4   ounces reduced-fat cheddar cheese with jalapeño peppers, shredded (about 1 cup; such as Cabot)
4   lime wedges

1 Heat chicken according to package directions.

2 Combine oil, lime juice, and salt in a medium bowl, stirring with a whisk. Add slaw, green onions, and cilantro; toss to coat.

3 Preheat broiler.

4 Place tostada shells on a baking sheet. Spread ¼ cup black beans on each tostada shell; top each with a scant ½ cup chicken, and sprinkle with about ¼ cup cheese. Broil 1 to 2 minutes or until cheese melts and begins to brown. Top each tostada with about ½ cup slaw. Serve immediately with lime wedges.

SERVING SIZE: 1 tostada

CALORIES 325; FAT 14.4g (sat 5.3g, mono 5.4g, poly 3.2g); PROTEIN 23g; CARB 26g; FIBER 5g; SUGARS 2g (est. added sugars 0g); CHOL 46mg; IRON 2mg; SODIUM 817mg; CALC 240mg

PARMESAN-CRUSTED CHICKEN CUTLETS
OVER LEMON-BROCCOLI PASTA TOSS

Instead of breading your own chicken, check your market's poultry department for prebreaded and seasoned cutlets. Just be sure to ask what's in the breading as some can be high in sodium.

SERVES 4 • HANDS-ON TIME: 14 MIN. • TOTAL TIME: 19 MIN.

1½ cups uncooked rotini (corkscrew pasta)
2 cups broccoli florets
2 tablespoons olive oil, divided
4 (3-ounce) prebreaded Parmesan-crusted chicken cutlets (such as Fresh Market)
Cooking spray
1 tablespoon butter
1 small garlic clove, minced
¼ teaspoon grated lemon rind
1 tablespoon fresh lemon juice
⅜ teaspoon salt
⅛ teaspoon freshly ground black pepper
1 ounce fresh Parmesan cheese, grated (about ¼ cup)
1 tablespoon chopped fresh parsley

❶ Cook pasta according to package directions, omitting salt and fat and adding broccoli during last 3 minutes of cooking time. Drain; transfer to a medium bowl, and keep warm.

❷ While pasta cooks, heat 1 tablespoon oil in a large nonstick skillet over medium-high heat. Add chicken cutlets to pan; cook 2 to 3 minutes or until golden brown. Coat chicken with cooking spray; turn chicken over. Cook an additional 2 to 3 minutes or until browned and done.

❸ Heat remaining 1 tablespoon oil and butter in a small saucepan over medium heat until butter melts; add garlic, and sauté 1 minute. Remove from heat and stir in lemon rind, lemon juice, salt, and pepper. Pour sauce over pasta mixture, tossing to coat.

❹ Place pasta mixture on each of 4 plates; sprinkle evenly with cheese. Top each serving with 1 chicken cutlet, and sprinkle evenly with parsley.

SERVING SIZE: 1 cup pasta mixture, 1 chicken cutlet, 1 tablespoon cheese, and ¾ teaspoon parsley

CALORIES 447; FAT 14.6g (sat 4.8g, mono 6.7g, poly 1.2g); PROTEIN 34g; CARB 39g; FIBER 3g; SUGARS 3g (est. added sugars 1g); CHOL 99mg; IRON 2mg; SODIUM 590mg; CALC 100mg

PEANUTTY CHICKEN NOODLES WITH SNOW PEAS

Snow peas and carrots cook along with the pasta, making this a one-pot meal with rich Asian flavors.

SERVES 8 • HANDS-ON TIME: 15 MIN. • TOTAL TIME: 15 MIN.

8 ounces uncooked soba noodles
5 ounces snow peas, halved diagonally
    (1½ cups)
1 cup matchstick-cut carrots
2½ cups shredded warm
    rotisserie chicken
½ cup thinly sliced green onions

½ cup bottled peanut sauce
    (such as House of Tsang)
3 tablespoons water
1 tablespoon lower-sodium soy sauce
1 tablespoon unseasoned rice vinegar
¼ cup chopped unsalted
    dry-roasted peanuts

1 Cook soba noodles according to package directions, omitting salt and fat, adding snow peas and carrots during last 2 minutes of cooking time. Drain; transfer to a large bowl. Add chicken and green onions.

2 Combine peanut sauce and next 3 ingredients (through rice vinegar), stirring with a whisk. Pour over noodle mixture, tossing to coat. Place noodle mixture on each of 8 plates; top each serving with peanuts.

SERVING SIZE: 1 cup noodle mixture and 1½ teaspoons peanuts

CALORIES 260; FAT 8.2g (sat 1.2g, mono 3.4g, poly 1.7g); PROTEIN 19g; CARB 27g; FIBER 3g; SUGARS 5g (est. added sugars 2g); CHOL 50mg; IRON 2mg; SODIUM 781mg; CALC 20mg

THAI CURRY-LIME SOUP
WITH CHICKEN AND VEGETABLES

Healthy, comforting, and full of flavor, this bright Asian soup is brimming with fresh herbs and a subtle heat. Serve with fish sauce—made from anchovies, salt, and water—so guests can season to taste.

SERVES 8 • HANDS-ON TIME: 19 MIN. • TOTAL TIME: 19 MIN.

➡ **Savvy Shortcuts**
Skip the sauté pan: Use 3 cups packaged Asian slaw mix instead of the mushrooms, carrots, and bok choy, and let the slaw mix wilt in the hot broth.

2 (20-ounce) packages frozen Thai curry and lime broth (such as Nona Lim)
2 cups water
1 teaspoon dark sesame oil
1 cup sliced shiitake mushroom caps
⅓ cup sliced green onions
4 baby bok choy, coarsely chopped
2 cups shredded rotisserie chicken breast
1 cup refrigerated preshredded carrot
1 (14.8-ounce) package frozen pad see ew noodles, thawed (such as Nona Lim)
¼ cup chopped fresh cilantro
2 tablespoons basil leaves
1 small jalapeño pepper, thinly sliced (optional)

❶ Bring broth and 2 cups water to a boil; reduce heat until barely simmering. Cover and simmer about 6 minutes.

❷ Heat a large nonstick skillet over medium high-heat. Add sesame oil; swirl to coat. Add mushrooms and green onions; stir-fry 3 minutes. Add bok choy; stir-fry 3 minutes or until vegetables are crisp-tender.

❸ Add chicken, carrot, and noodles to broth. Return to a simmer, and cook 3 minutes or until thoroughly heated.

❹ Place noodle mixture in each of 8 warm bowls using tongs. Top noodle mixture in each bowl with bok choy mixture. Ladle broth into each bowl. Top each serving with cilantro and basil. Sprinkle with jalapeño pepper slices, if desired. Serve immediately.

SERVING SIZE: ¾ cup noodle mixture, ⅓ cup bok choy mixture, ½ cup broth, 1½ teaspoons cilantro, and ¾ teaspoon basil
CALORIES 283; **FAT** 17.8g (sat 5.6g, mono 3.2g, poly 3.2g); **PROTEIN** 11g; **CARB** 22g; **FIBER** 2g; **SUGARS** 5g (est. added sugars 1g); **CHOL** 31mg; **IRON** 2mg; **SODIUM** 470mg; **CALC** 85mg

MEDITERRANEAN CHICKEN ORZO

The deli and hot bar do most of the work in this warm-weather chicken pasta dish. You'll have to invest just 10 minutes to make a fresh vinaigrette and round out the rest of the ingredients that make the entire plate pop.

SERVES 6 • HANDS-ON TIME: 10 MIN. • TOTAL TIME: 10 MIN.

2   tablespoons sherry vinegar
1½ tablespoons olive oil
2   teaspoons chopped fresh oregano
½   teaspoon grated lemon rind
½   teaspoon Dijon mustard
¼   teaspoon freshly ground black pepper
3   cups premade orzo salad with spinach, grape tomatoes, and pine nuts (1 pound 3 ounces; such as Whole Foods)

2   cups shredded rotisserie chicken
¾   cup drained canned quartered artichoke hearts in water, coarsely chopped
⅔   cup chopped celery or fennel bulb

1 Combine first 6 ingredients in a small bowl; stir with a whisk.

2 Combine orzo salad and remaining ingredients in a large bowl. Drizzle with vinaigrette; toss until coated.

SERVING SIZE: 1 cup

CALORIES 258; FAT 13.6g (sat 2.8g, mono 6.1g, poly 1.2g); PROTEIN 15g; CARB 21g; FIBER 3g; SUGARS 3g (est. added sugars 0g); CHOL 47mg; IRON 0mg; SODIUM 583mg; CALC 13mg

CHICKEN KEBABS
WITH PITA BREAD SALAD

It's amazing how quickly fresh mint, feta, and a little lemon juice can turn chicken and vegetables into a lively Greek meal.

SERVES 6 • HANDS-ON TIME: 8 MIN. • TOTAL TIME: 18 MIN.

6   (10-ounce) uncooked premade chicken-vegetable kebabs

2   (2.8-ounce) Mediterranean-style white flatbreads (such as Toufayan)

Olive oil-flavored cooking spray

2   cups premade tomato-cucumber salad, coarsely chopped (such as Whole Foods)

1   ounce crumbled feta cheese (about ¼ cup)

¼   cup chopped fresh mint leaves

½   cup plain fat-free Greek yogurt

1   tablespoon fresh lemon juice

1   teaspoon ground cumin

1 Preheat grill to medium-high heat.

2 Coat kebabs and flatbreads with cooking spray. Place kebabs on grill rack coated with cooking spray; grill 5 minutes. Turn kebabs over; add flatbreads to grill rack. Grill 3 to 5 minutes or until chicken is done and flatbreads are crisp. Remove kebabs and flatbreads from grill; keep warm.

3 Drain tomato salad, reserving 3 tablespoons liquid. Tear flatbreads into ½-inch pieces, and place in a large bowl. Add tomato salad, cheese, mint, and reserved salad liquid; toss until flatbread is moist. Let stand 5 minutes.

4 Combine yogurt, lemon juice, and cumin in a small bowl; stirring with a whisk. Serve sauce with kebabs.

SERVING SIZE: 1 kebab, ¾ cup salad, and 4 teaspoons yogurt sauce

CALORIES 411; FAT 12.7g (sat 3.4g, mono 3.4g, poly 1.5g); PROTEIN 46g; CARB 26g; FIBER 4g; SUGARS 8g (est. added sugars 3g); CHOL 136mg; IRON 5mg; SODIUM 348mg; CALC 102mg

THAI PEANUT CHICKEN CUTLETS
WITH RICE NOODLES

Quick-seared, peanut-crusted chicken bakes in the oven while rice noodles and carrots cook on the stovetop.

SERVES 6 • HANDS-ON TIME: 20 MIN. • TOTAL TIME: 33 MIN.

1 tablespoon canola oil, divided
2 (8-ounce) peanut-crusted chicken cutlets (such as Whole Foods)
½ pound uncooked wide rice sticks (rice-flour noodles)
1 cup matchstick-cut carrots
⅓ cup spicy peanut sauce (such as House of Tsang)
2 tablespoons water
1½ tablespoons rice vinegar
1½ cups diagonally cut snow peas
½ cup diagonally cut green onions
¼ cup chopped fresh cilantro
6 basil sprigs
6 lime wedges

1 Preheat oven to 350°F.

2 Heat a large nonstick skillet over medium-high heat. Add 1 teaspoon oil to pan; swirl to coat. Add one-third of chicken; cook 1 minute on each side or until golden brown. Transfer chicken to a metal baking pan. Wipe drippings from skillet with a paper towel. Repeat procedure twice with remaining oil and chicken.

3 Bake chicken at 350°F for 8 minutes or until done. Cover and let stand 5 minutes. Cut chicken diagonally into slices.

4 While chicken cooks, cook noodles according package directions, adding carrots during last 1 minute of cooking time. Drain. Rinse with cold water; drain.

5 Combine peanut sauce, 2 tablespoons water, and rice vinegar in a large bowl. Add noodle mixture, snow peas, onions, and cilantro; toss gently. Place noodle mixture and chicken into each of 6 shallow bowls. Garnish with basil and lime.

SERVING SIZE: 1½ cups noodle mixture, about 2½ ounces chicken, 1 basil sprig, and 1 lime wedge

CALORIES 356; FAT 12.2g (sat 0.6g, mono 5.4g, poly 3.2g); PROTEIN 16g; CARB 41g; FIBER 2g; SUGARS 8g (est. added sugars 0g); CHOL 31mg; IRON 2mg; SODIUM 758mg; CALC 20mg

TURKEY BURGERS
WITH BLACK BEAN AND CORN PILAF

It's burger night, and buns aren't invited. Slather those patties with sweet-and-spicy sauce, and serve on whole-grain pilaf full of veggies.

SERVES 4 • HANDS-ON TIME: 25 MIN. • TOTAL TIME: 25 MIN.

½ cup unsalted ketchup
2 tablespoons chopped chipotle chiles, canned in adobo sauce
1 tablespoon fresh lime juice
1 tablespoon maple syrup
½ teaspoon onion powder
½ teaspoon ground cumin, divided
½ cup frozen fire-roasted corn
1 (15-ounce) can black beans, rinsed and drained
1 (10-ounce) package frozen, cooked quinoa and brown rice (such as Village Harvest)

4 (4-ounce) frozen turkey burgers (such as Applegate Farms)
Cooking spray
¼ teaspoon kosher salt
½ teaspoon freshly ground black pepper
¼ cup premade guacamole (such as Whole Foods)
2 tablespoons refrigerated fresh pico de gallo (such as Whole Foods)
¼ cup chopped fresh cilantro

❶ Combine first 5 ingredients and ¼ teaspoon cumin in a small saucepan; bring to a boil. Reduce heat; simmer 5 to 6 minutes or until thickened and reduced to ½ cup. Reserve ¼ cup sauce for basting; cover and keep remaining sauce warm.

❷ Combine corn, beans, and grain medley in a microwave-safe bowl, stirring well. Microwave, uncovered, at HIGH 3 minutes or until hot. Cover and keep warm.

❸ Preheat a heavy grill pan. Lightly coat turkey burgers and grill pan with cooking spray. Sprinkle burgers with salt, pepper, and remaining ¼ teaspoon cumin; grill 6 minutes. Turn burgers over; grill 4 minutes. Brush top of each burger with 1 tablespoon reserved sauce. Grill an additional 2 minutes or until a thermometer registers 165°F.

❹ Place pilaf on each of 4 plates; top each serving with a burger, sauce, guacamole, pico de gallo, and cilantro.

SERVING SIZE: 1 cup pilaf, 1 burger, 1 tablespoon sauce, 1 tablespoon guacamole, 1½ teaspoons pico de gallo, and 1 tablespoon cilantro

CALORIES 461; FAT 12.4g (sat 2.8g, mono 4.3g, poly 2.5g); PROTEIN 26g; CARB 62g; FIBER 8g; SUGARS 13g (est. added sugars 6g); CHOL 60mg; IRON 3mg; SODIUM 630mg; CALC 63mg

TURKEY, MUSHROOM, AND WILD RICE SOUP

Block off two nights on your weekly meal plan for this delicious soup that serves four twice. If you can't find rotisserie turkey breast, substitute rotisserie chicken.

SERVES 9 • HANDS-ON TIME: 25 MIN. • TOTAL TIME: 25 MIN.

2   tablespoons unsalted butter
¾   cup diced celery
¾   cup matchstick-cut carrots, diced
1   (8-ounce) container refrigerated prechopped onion
1   (8-ounce) package sliced cremini mushrooms
1.1 ounces all-purpose flour (about ¼ cup)
⅛   teaspoon salt

¼   teaspoon freshly ground black pepper
5   cups unsalted chicken stock (such as Kitchen Basics)
3   cups shredded rotisserie turkey breast
1   (8.8-ounce) pouch precooked long-grain and wild rice
½   cup half-and-half
3   tablespoons chopped fresh parsley

1 Melt butter in a Dutch oven over medium-high heat. Add celery, carrots, and onion; sauté 6 minutes or until beginning to soften. Add mushrooms; cook, stirring frequently, 5 minutes or until tender.

2 Lightly spoon flour into a dry measuring cup; level with a knife. Sprinkle flour, salt, and pepper over vegetable mixture; cook, stirring constantly, 1 minute. Gradually stir in chicken stock, scraping pan to loosen browned bits. Cover; bring to a boil.

3 Stir in turkey and rice; cover, reduce heat, and simmer 5 minutes or until vegetables are tender and soup is thickened. Remove from heat; stir in half-and-half.

4 Ladle soup into each of 9 bowls; sprinkle each serving with parsley.

SERVING SIZE: about 1 cup soup and 1 teaspoon parsley

CALORIES 214; FAT 8.4g (sat 2.9g, mono 2.2g, poly 1.3g); PROTEIN 20g; CARB 16g; FIBER 2g; SUGARS 3g (est. added sugars 0g); CHOL 43mg; IRON 1mg; SODIUM 364mg; CALC 49mg;

Fast Freeze

Soup is perfect for popping in the freezer and heating up for a simple supper when you're short on time. If you have any leftovers, freeze them for later, or better yet, double the recipe so you'll have an entire homemade batch ready for a night when you have no time to cook.

ROASTED TURKEY
WITH WHEAT BERRY AND BRUSSELS SPROUTS SALAD

In a few minutes, pomegranate-cranberry juice becomes a rich, fruity glaze that takes deli turkey to the next level.

SERVES 4 • HANDS-ON TIME: 14 MIN. • TOTAL TIME: 22 MIN.

Fast Freeze

Turn leftover fruit juice into ice pops, or freeze it into cubes and make your iced tea cool in more ways than you can imagine.

¾ cup pomegranate-cranberry juice
1 (1-pound, 9-ounce) roasted whole deli turkey breast (such as Whole Foods)
½ teaspoon grated lemon rind
2 tablespoons fresh lemon juice
1 tablespoon olive oil
1 teaspoon chopped fresh thyme
½ teaspoon honey
¼ teaspoon kosher salt
¼ teaspoon freshly ground black pepper
1 (10-ounce) package frozen whole-grain medley with wheat berries, barley, cranberries, and almonds, thawed (such as Village Harvest)
1 (9-ounce) package preshredded Brussels sprouts (4 cups)

1 Preheat oven to 350°F.

2 Bring pomegranate juice to a boil in a small saucepan over medium-high heat. Reduce heat, and simmer, uncovered, 6 minutes or until syrupy and reduced to about 3 tablespoons.

3 Place turkey on a foil-lined baking sheet. Spoon syrup over turkey. Bake at 350°F for 6 minutes or until thoroughly heated.

4 Combine lemon rind and next 6 ingredients (through pepper) in a large bowl. Add grain medley and Brussels sprouts; toss to coat.

5 Cut turkey into slices, reserving pan juices. Drizzle turkey with pan juices, and serve with grain salad.

SERVING SIZE: 4¼ ounces turkey and about 1 cup salad

CALORIES 468; FAT 16.4g (sat 1.6g, mono 6.9g, poly 3.5g); PROTEIN 46g; CARB 38g; FIBER 6g; SUGARS 11g (est. added sugars 5g); CHOL 90mg; IRON 2mg; SODIUM 321mg; CALC 48mg

ROAST BEEF–BLUE CHEESE SANDWICHES

Cooked beef tenderloin would also work well in this restaurant-quality sandwich with a tangy cheese spread. Bake frozen sweet potato fries while preparing the sandwiches to round out the meal.

SERVES 4 • HANDS-ON TIME: 11 MIN. • TOTAL TIME: 11 MIN.

¼ cup canola mayonnaise
¼ cup light sour cream
1 ounce crumbled blue cheese (about ¼ cup)
½ teaspoon grated lemon rind
⅛ teaspoon freshly ground black pepper
8 (1-ounce) slices hearty white bread, toasted (such as Fresh Market Italian Bread)

12 ounces thinly sliced lower-sodium deli roast beef (such as Boar's Head)
½ cup roasted tomatoes, coarsely chopped
⅔ cup sliced grilled red onion
2 cups loosely packed arugula

1 Combine first 5 ingredients in a small bowl. Spread about 1½ tablespoons mayonnaise mixture on 1 side of each bread slice; top each of 4 slices with 3 ounces beef, 2 tablespoons tomatoes, about 3 tablespoons red onion, and ½ cup arugula. Cover with remaining 4 bread slices, mayonnaise mixture side down.

SERVING SIZE: 1 sandwich

CALORIES 422; FAT 17.1g (sat 3.9g, mono 4.2g, poly 1.7g); PROTEIN 30g; CARB 35g; FIBER 4g; SUGARS 6g (est. added sugars 1g); CHOL 64mg; IRON 3mg; SODIUM 881mg; CALC 89mg;

Eat Now & Later

Make an extra sandwich, and butter the outside of the bread. Grill quickly, cool to room temperature, refrigerate, and enjoy for lunch the next day.

PICADILLO BURRITOS

Typically served over rice, picadillo is a fragrant Cuban dish of beef, raisins, and olives. Here we transform it into a burrito filling topped with lettuce, avocado, and cheese. Serve with rice and black beans for a heartier meal.

SERVES 6 • HANDS-ON TIME: 21 MIN. • TOTAL TIME: 21 MIN.

1   pound ground sirloin
1   cup chopped onion
2   garlic cloves, minced
⅓   cup chopped green olives
¼   cup raisins
1   teaspoon ground cumin
¼   teaspoon ground cinnamon
¼   teaspoon salt
¼   teaspoon freshly ground black pepper

1   (14.5-ounce) can unsalted diced tomatoes, undrained
6   (8-inch) fat-free flour tortillas (such as La Banderita)
2   cups bagged shredded iceberg lettuce
1   small avocado, peeled and thinly sliced
1.5 ounces crumbled Cotija cheese (about 6 tablespoons)

❶ Cook first 3 ingredients in a large nonstick skillet over medium-high heat 6 minutes or until beef is browned, stirring to crumble. Drain; return to pan. Stir in olives and next 6 ingredients (through tomatoes). Bring to a boil; reduce heat, and simmer, uncovered, 5 minutes or until slightly thickened.

❷ Heat tortillas according to package directions. Spoon about ½ cup beef mixture into center of each tortilla. Top with ⅓ cup lettuce, one-sixth of avocado, and 1 tablespoon cheese. Roll up; secure with wooden picks.

SERVING SIZE: 1 burrito

CALORIES 364; **FAT** 14.3g (sat 4.8g, mono 6.9g, poly 1.1g); **PROTEIN** 22g; **CARB** 33g; **FIBER** 9g; **SUGARS** 8g (est. added sugars 1g); **CHOL** 57mg; **IRON** 3mg; **SODIUM** 606mg; **CALC** 213mg;

QUICK BEEF PHO

Pronounced "fuh," this Vietnamese noodle soup comes together quicker—and tastes fresher—than takeout ever could. Freezing the meat for a few minutes makes it easier to slice thinly.

SERVES 6 • HANDS-ON TIME: 10 MIN. • TOTAL TIME: 25 MIN.

- 8 ounces rice noodles
- 12 ounces flank steak
- 6 cups beef stock
- 2 star anise
- 1 (½-inch) piece peeled fresh ginger, cut into 4 slices
- 1½ cups bean sprouts
- ¾ cup sliced green onions (about 5 medium)
- ½ cup basil leaves
- ½ cup cilantro leaves
- 2 red jalapeño peppers, thinly sliced
- 6 lime wedges

1 Soak rice noodles according to package directions; drain. Freeze flank steak 15 minutes.

2 Combine beef stock, anise, and ginger in a large saucepan or Dutch oven. Bring to a boil; cover, reduce heat, and simmer 15 minutes.

3 Cut steak diagonally across grain into ⅛-inch-thick slices. Remove ginger and anise from broth using a slotted spoon. Add rice noodles to broth; return to a simmer. Add beef; remove from heat. Ladle broth mixture into each of 6 bowls. Top each serving with bean sprouts, green onions, basil, cilantro, jalapeño, and a lime wedge.

SERVING SIZE: 1⅓ cups broth mixture, ¼ cup bean sprouts, 2 tablespoons green onions, 4 teaspoons basil, 4 teaspoons cilantro, 2 teaspoons jalapeño, and 1 lime wedge

CALORIES 245; FAT 3.2g (sat 1.2g, mono 1.1g, poly 0.2g); PROTEIN 16g; CARB 37g; FIBER 1g; SUGARS 4g (est. added sugars 0g); CHOL 35mg; IRON 3mg; SODIUM 537mg; CALC 54mg

Savvy Shortcuts

If you can find ready-made pho broth (such as Nona Lim or Pacific) in either the freezer section or soup section at specialty foods stores, use it in place of the beef stock, anise, and ginger.

SHEPHERD'S PIE

Made with precut veggies and premade mashers, this stick-to-your-ribs meal won't leave you stuck in the kitchen for hours. If you prefer lamb, brown the meat, but drain off the fat before stirring in the flour.

SERVES 8 • HANDS-ON TIME: 16 MIN. • TOTAL TIME: 20 MIN.

Fast Freeze

Freeze cup-sized portions of any leftover beef broth, and use them later as a base for risotto, sautéed mushrooms, or a meaty pasta sauce.

1½ pounds ground sirloin
1 cup refrigerated prechopped onion
1 cup matchstick-cut carrots, coarsely chopped
1 garlic clove, minced
2 tablespoons all-purpose flour
¼ teaspoon salt
¼ teaspoon freshly ground black pepper
1⅓ cups lower-sodium beef broth

¾ cup frozen petite green peas
1 (24-ounce) package refrigerated mashed potatoes (such as Simply Potatoes Traditional Mashed Potatoes)
Cooking spray
2 ounces shredded reduced-fat sharp cheddar cheese (about ½ cup)
1 tablespoon chopped fresh parsley

1 Preheat broiler.

2 Cook first 4 ingredients in a large nonstick skillet over medium-high heat 10 minutes or until meat is browned and vegetables are tender, stirring to crumble meat. Sprinkle meat mixture with flour, salt, and pepper; cook, stirring constantly, 1 minute. Stir in broth; bring to a boil and cook, stirring constantly, 1 minute or until thickened. Stir in peas.

3 Heat mashed potatoes in microwave according to package directions.

4 Spoon beef mixture into an 11 x 7-inch broiler-safe ceramic baking dish coated with cooking spray. Top mixture with mashed potatoes; sprinkle with cheese.

5 Broil 4 minutes or until topping is browned. Sprinkle with parsley.

SERVING SIZE: about 1 cup

CALORIES 296; FAT 14.5g (sat 7.2g, mono 4.9g, poly 0.6g); PROTEIN 22g; CARB 18g; FIBER 3g; SUGARS 3g (est. added sugars 0g); CHOL 75mg; IRON 3mg; SODIUM 572mg; CALC 101mg;

SHREDDED BEEF TACOS
WITH SALSA VERDE

Combine prepared beef roast with fresh ingredients for a family-friendly taco in minutes. If you find barbecue beef brisket on the hot bar, snag that instead. And if you have a gas stove, you can toast the tortillas over the flame.

SERVES 6 • HANDS-ON TIME: 15 MIN. • TOTAL TIME: 15 MIN.

2 (15-ounce) packages refrigerated beef roast au jus (such as Hormel)
12 (6-inch) corn tortillas, warmed
¾ cup salsa verde
3 cups bagged shredded iceberg lettuce
¾ cup chopped white onion
3 ounces crumbled queso fresco (about ¾ cup)
¼ cup chopped fresh cilantro
6 lime wedges

1 Microwave beef roast according to package directions until thoroughly heated. Drain, discarding juices. Shred beef using 2 forks.

2 Place ¼ cup beef on each tortilla; top each with 1 tablespoon salsa, ½ cup lettuce, 1 tablespoon onion, 1 tablespoon cheese, and 1 teaspoon cilantro. Fold tortillas in half. Serve with lime wedges.

SERVING SIZE: 2 tacos and 1 lime wedge

CALORIES 315; FAT 11.3g (sat 4.5g, mono 2.9g, poly 1.2g); PROTEIN 22g; CARB 31g; FIBER 4g; SUGARS 8g (est. added sugars 2g); CHOL 57mg; IRON 0mg; SODIUM 684mg; CALC 98mg

Eat Now & Later

Beef taco leftovers are just the beginning of another meal. Top a premade pizza crust with salsa, add the beef mixture, top with shredded Monterey Jack cheese, and bake. Sprinkle with a little cilantro, slice, and serve.

HERBED LAMB CHOPS
WITH LEMONY ORZO SALAD

Ready-made orzo salad buys you a few extra minutes to spend creating a luscious rub full of fresh and dried herbs.

SERVES 4 • HANDS-ON TIME: 19 MIN. • TOTAL TIME: 24 MIN.

➡ **Savvy Shortcuts**

In a pinch, replace the homemade rub with 1 tablespoon salt-free Greek seasoning.

1   teaspoon coriander seeds
1   teaspoon fennel seeds
1   lemon
1½ tablespoons olive oil
1½ teaspoons chopped fresh thyme
1   teaspoon chopped fresh rosemary
¼   teaspoon kosher salt
½   teaspoon freshly ground black pepper
6   roasted garlic cloves, minced
4   (4-ounce) lamb loin chops, trimmed
Cooking spray
3   cups premade orzo salad with spinach and grape tomatoes (such as Whole Foods)
6   lemon wedges

❶ Preheat broiler.

❷ Place coriander seeds and fennel seeds in a small skillet; cook over medium heat 2 to 3 minutes or until seeds are lightly browned, shaking pan frequently. Cool to room temperature.

❸ Grate rind and squeeze juice from lemon to measure 1½ teaspoons rind and 1 teaspoon juice. Set aside.

❹ Place seeds in a small heavy-duty zip-top plastic bag. Crush seeds using a meat mallet or small heavy skillet. Combine crushed seeds, ½ teaspoon lemon rind, oil, and next 5 ingredients (through garlic) in a small bowl. Rub mixture evenly over lamb chops. Place lamb chops on a broiler pan coated with cooking spray. Broil 3 to 4 minutes on each side or until desired degree of doneness.

❺ Combine lemon juice, orzo salad, and remaining 1 teaspoon lemon rind; toss well. Serve lamb chops with orzo salad and lemon wedges.

SERVING SIZE: 1 lamb chop, ¾ cup orzo salad, and 1 lemon wedge

CALORIES 438; FAT 23.1g (sat 5.4g, mono 10.4g, poly 1.9g); PROTEIN 30g; CARB 29g; FIBER 4g; SUGARS 3g (est. added sugars 0g); CHOL 82mg; IRON 2mg; SODIUM 644g; CALC 27mg

PORK FRIED RICE

The genius of frozen cooked rice is revealed in this recipe: Fried rice always tastes best when the grains start out cold. Simply spread on a baking sheet, and thaw at room temperature while prepping the other ingredients.

SERVES 5 • HANDS-ON TIME: 20 MIN. • TOTAL TIME: 20 MIN.

- 2 tablespoons lower-sodium soy sauce
- 1 tablespoon unseasoned rice vinegar
- 2 teaspoons dark sesame oil
- 2 tablespoons peanut oil, divided
- 2 (3-ounce) smoked boneless pork chops, cut into ½-inch pieces (1¼ cups; such as Smithfield)
- ½ cup chopped green onions
- ¾ cup matchstick-cut carrots, coarsely chopped
- 1 head baby bok choy, halved lengthwise and thinly sliced (1¾ cups)
- 3 cups frozen cooked brown rice, thawed
- ¾ cup frozen petite green peas
- 2 large eggs, lightly beaten
- ½ cup chopped green onion tops

1 Combine first 3 ingredients in a small bowl, stirring with a whisk.

2 Heat a wok or large nonstick skillet over high heat. Add 1 tablespoon peanut oil to pan; swirl to coat. Add pork; stir-fry 2 minutes or until browned. Remove from pan.

3 Add remaining 1 tablespoon peanut oil to pan; swirl to coat. Add chopped green onions, carrots, and bok choy; stir-fry 2 to 3 minutes or until tender. Stir in rice and peas; stir-fry 2 minutes or until rice is hot.

4 Move rice and vegetables to edge of pan, creating a well in center. Pour egg into well; stir-fry 30 seconds or until scrambled. Stir in pork, soy sauce mixture, and green onion tops; remove from heat. Serve immediately.

SERVING SIZE: 1 cup

CALORIES 310; FAT 12.1g (sat 2.5g, mono 4g, poly 3g); PROTEIN 13g; CARB 38g; FIBER 3g; SUGARS 5g (est. added sugars 0g); CHOL 93mg; IRON 2mg; SODIUM 668mg; CALC 49mg

Eat Now & Later

When the chips are down, it's time to make nachos! Top cheese-covered chips with the leftover pork mixture, and broil for a few minutes until bubbly.

PULLED PORK SUMMER ROLLS
WITH ASIAN BROCCOLI SLAW

Perfect for a picnic, these fresh and crunchy rolls let you bring the barbecue to the party and leave the forks at home.

SERVES 8 • HANDS-ON TIME: 25 MIN. • TOTAL TIME: 25 MIN.

Eat Now & Later

A few leftover rolls might not make an entire meal for your family, but they'll add plenty of protein to a big lunch salad full of Bibb lettuce, carrots, slivered almonds, and cabbage with sesame dressing.

2   tablespoons canola mayonnaise
½   teaspoon dark sesame oil
2   teaspoons rice vinegar, divided
1   (12-ounce) package broccoli coleslaw
¼   cup thinly sliced green onions
1   tablespoon black sesame seeds
2   tablespoons hoisin sauce

8   ounces smoked pulled pork, warmed
16   (8-inch) round rice paper sheets
16   large basil leaves (½ cup)
16   small cilantro sprigs (½ cup)
¼   cup barbecue sauce (such as Sticky Fingers Memphis Original)

1 Combine mayonnaise, sesame oil, and 1 teaspoon rice vinegar in a large bowl, stirring until blended. Add coleslaw, green onions, and sesame seeds; toss to coat.

2 Combine hoisin sauce and remaining 1 teaspoon rice vinegar in a medium bowl, stirring with a whisk. Add pork; toss to coat. Fill a shallow dish with water to a depth of 1 inch. Add rice paper sheets, 2 at a time, to water; soak 1 minute or until softened.

3 Place a damp paper towel on a work surface. Place 2 softened rice paper sheets, slightly overlapping, on paper towel. Place 2 basil leaves and 2 cilantro sprigs on bottom third of 1 sheet. Top with 1 ounce pork and ⅓ cup slaw. Fold in sides of rice papers; roll up, gently pressing seam to seal. Place roll, seam side down, on a serving platter; cut roll in half, and cover with a damp paper towel to prevent drying. Repeat procedure with remaining rice paper sheets, basil, cilantro, pork, and slaw.

4 Serve rolls with remaining slaw and barbecue sauce for dipping.

SERVING SIZE: 1 roll, about 2½ tablespoons slaw, and 1½ teaspoons sauce

CALORIES 199; FAT 7.5g (sat 2.1g, mono 3.4g, poly 1.8g); PROTEIN 11g; CARB 21g; FIBER 2g; SUGARS 5g (est. added sugars 2g); CHOL 25mg; IRON 1mg; SODIUM 256mg; CALC 40mg

SMOKED PORK AND PEPPER PIZZA

Smoked chicken works just as well on this peppery pie. Look for sliced peppers and red onion either at your grocer's salad bar or packaged in the produce section.

SERVES 6 • HANDS-ON TIME: 7 MIN. • TOTAL TIME: 24 MIN.

1 pound refrigerated fresh pizza dough, at room temperature (such as Whole Foods)

2 teaspoons olive oil

1 cup refrigerated sliced tricolor bell peppers

¾ cup thinly sliced red onion

⅓ cup spicy barbecue sauce (such as Stubb's)

2 cups shredded smoked pork (such as Bishop's)

4 ounces reduced-fat cheddar cheese with jalapeño peppers, shredded (about 1 cup; such as Cabot)

1 tablespoon coarsely chopped fresh cilantro

1 Preheat oven to 450°F.

2 Roll or press pizza dough into a 14-inch circle on a 16-inch round sheet of parchment paper on a large baking sheet. Place a large pizza pan in preheated oven. Heat 4 minutes or until hot.

3 While pan preheats, heat a large nonstick skillet over medium-high heat. Add oil; swirl to coat. Add bell pepper and onion; sauté 4 minutes or just until tender and beginning to brown.

4 Spread barbecue sauce evenly over pizza dough, leaving a 1-inch border. Top with pork, pepper mixture, and cheese. Slide pizza and parchment paper onto preheated pan; place on bottom rack in oven.

5 Bake at 450°F for 17 minutes or until golden brown. Sprinkle with cilantro. Cut into 12 slices.

SERVING SIZE: 2 slices

CALORIES 377; FAT 13g (sat 4.9g, mono 1.9g, poly 0.5g); PROTEIN 22g; CARB 41g; FIBER 6g; SUGARS 2g (est. added sugars 1g); CHOL 43mg; IRON 2mg; SODIUM 574mg; CALC 156mg

Eat Now & Later

Double the pizza dough, and reinvent the leftovers later as breadsticks covered in olive oil and Parmesan cheese; quick dinner rolls; or a calzone stuffed with leftover Teriyaki Pork Tenderloin filling (page 61).

STIR-FRIED PORK AND ASIAN GREENS

Bagged Asian greens and fresh pineapple from the salad bar are quick go-tos for this easy pork stir-fry.

SERVES 4 • HANDS-ON TIME: 25 MIN. • TOTAL TIME: 25 MIN.

½ (20-ounce) package frozen jasmine rice (such as 365 Organic)
⅓ cup hoisin sauce
¼ cup water
1 tablespoon rice vinegar
2 teaspoons canola oil, divided
3 (4-ounce) boneless center-cut loin pork chops (about ½ inch thick), trimmed and thinly sliced
2 teaspoons sesame oil
1 tablespoon grated peeled fresh ginger
2 garlic cloves, minced
1 cup snow peas, trimmed and cut into 1-inch pieces
1 (10.7-ounce) bag chopped Asian blend greens (such as Dole Chopped Asian Blend)
¾ cup chopped fresh pineapple
Sliced green onions (optional)
Cilantro leaves (optional)

1 Prepare rice according to package directions.

2 Combine hoisin sauce, water, and vinegar, stirring with a whisk.

3 Heat a large nonstick skillet over medium-high heat. Add 1 teaspoon canola oil to pan; swirl to coat. Add half of pork; cook 3 minutes or until lightly browned. Transfer to a bowl. Repeat with remaining 1 teaspoon canola oil and remaining half of pork.

4 Heat pan over medium-high heat. Add sesame oil; swirl to coat. Add ginger and garlic; cook 1 minute or until fragrant. Stir in snow peas and greens; sauté 2 minutes or until crisp-tender. Stir in pork, pineapple, and hoisin mixture. Bring to a boil; cook, uncovered, 1 minute or until sauce thickens. Serve pork mixture over rice; sprinkle with green onions and cilantro, if desired.

SERVING SIZE: 1¼ cups pork mixture and ½ cup rice

CALORIES 425; FAT 17.3g (sat 4.8g, mono 7.9g, poly 3.3g); PROTEIN 21g; CARB 45g; FIBER 3g; SUGARS 12g (est. added sugars 5g); CHOL 52mg; IRON 2mg; SODIUM 402mg; CALC 61mg

TERIYAKI PORK TENDERLOIN MU SHU WRAPS

Squeezing dinner in between this and that? These perfectly portable wraps make for a meaty meal on the move.

SERVES 10 • HANDS-ON TIME: 17 MIN. • TOTAL TIME: 17 MIN.

1   (1-pound) package teriyaki-marinated pork tenderloin

1   teaspoon dark sesame oil

1   (8-ounce) package presliced exotic mushroom blend (such as shiitake, cremini, and oyster), chopped (such as Publix Gourmet Blend)

Cooking spray

1   (14-ounce) package cabbage-and-carrot coleslaw with red cabbage

1   (3-ounce) package presliced green onions

6   tablespoons hoisin sauce

2   tablespoons water

1   tablespoon rice vinegar

10 (8-inch) fat-free flour tortillas (such as La Banderita)

Lime wedges (optional)

1 Drain and rinse pork; pat dry with paper towels. Cut pork crosswise into ½-inch-thick slices. Heat a large nonstick skillet over medium-high heat. Add sesame oil; swirl to coat. Add pork slices; cook 4 minutes on each side or until browned. Remove from pan. Add mushrooms to pan; coat with cooking spray. Cook, stirring frequently, 3 minutes or until lightly browned. Add coleslaw and green onions; cook, stirring frequently, 3 minutes or until vegetables are slightly tender. Add hoisin sauce, 2 tablespoons water, and rice vinegar, tossing to coat. Remove from heat; cover and keep warm.

2 Cut pork slices into julienne strips, reserving accumulated juices. Stir pork and juices into vegetable mixture.

3 Spoon about ½ cup pork mixture onto the bottom third of each tortilla. Fold in edges of tortillas; roll up. Serve with lime wedges, if desired.

SERVING SIZE: 1 wrap

CALORIES 205; FAT 2.4g (sat 0.6g, mono 1g, poly 0.7g); PROTEIN 14g; CARB 29g; FIBER 7g; SUGARS 6g (est. added sugars 2g); CHOL 21mg; IRON 2mg; SODIUM 502mg; CALC 127mg

GRILLED SALMON
WITH WHOLE-GRAIN PILAF

Send lemon and asparagus on a delicious double date with grilled salmon and grains, and have dinner on the table in less than 10 minutes.

SERVES 6 • HANDS-ON TIME: 7 MIN. • TOTAL TIME: 7 MIN.

1   (13-ounce) package frozen ancient-grain medley (such as Engine 2)
2   tablespoons water
1   pound asparagus spears
Cooking spray
¼   teaspoon kosher salt
¼   cup chopped fresh parsley

½   teaspoon grated lemon rind
2   tablespoons fresh lemon juice
1   tablespoon extra-virgin olive oil
2   cups grape tomatoes, halved
4   (6-ounce) pregrilled salmon fillets (such as Whole Foods)
6   lemon wedges

❶ Combine grain medley and 2 tablespoons water in a large microwave-safe bowl. Cover with plastic wrap; vent. Microwave at HIGH 2 minutes. Keep warm.

❷ Snap off tough ends of asparagus; cut diagonally into ¾-inch pieces. Heat a large nonstick skillet over medium-high heat. Add asparagus to pan. Coat asparagus with cooking spray; sprinkle with salt. Sauté over medium-high heat 4 minutes or until asparagus is crisp-tender.

❸ Add parsley and next 3 ingredients (through oil) to grain medley; toss well. Add asparagus and tomatoes; toss.

❹ Place salmon on a microwave-safe plate. Cover with wax paper. Microwave at HIGH 1 minute or until thoroughly heated. Break salmon into large pieces using a fork; gently fold into grain mixture. Place mixture on each of 6 plates. Serve with lemon wedges.

SERVING SIZE: 1½ cups salmon mixture and 1 lemon wedge

CALORIES 372; FAT 17.4g (sat 3.2g, mono 7g, poly 5.5g); PROTEIN 30g; CARB 22g; FIBER 4g; SUGARS 3g (est. added sugars 0g); CHOL 71mg; IRON 6mg; SODIUM 152mg; CALC 31mg

THAI COCONUT SHRIMP SOUP

Frozen Thai curry–lime broth and coconut milk serve as the base of this slightly spicy soup. Stir in a dash of fish sauce before serving for full flavor.

SERVES 8 • HANDS-ON TIME: 16 MIN. • TOTAL TIME: 16 MIN.

1 (8-ounce) package rice vermicelli
1 (20-ounce) package frozen Thai curry and lime broth, thawed (such as Nona Lim)
1 (13.5-ounce) can light coconut milk
1 tablespoon lemongrass paste
3 cups thinly sliced shiitake mushroom caps (½ pound)
1 pound medium shrimp, peeled and deveined
⅓ cup cilantro leaves
⅓ cup basil leaves
1½ tablespoons fresh lime juice
8 teaspoons Sriracha (hot chile sauce, such as Huy Fong)
8 lime wedges

1 Combine noodles and boiling water to cover in a large heatproof bowl. Let stand 8 minutes or until noodles are soft. Drain. Rinse with cold water; drain.

2 While noodles soften, combine broth, coconut milk, and lemongrass paste in a Dutch oven. Bring to a boil; reduce heat to medium. Stir in mushrooms; cook 5 minutes or until mushrooms are tender. Stir in shrimp; cook 3 minutes or until shrimp are done. Stir in noodles; cook 2 minutes or until thoroughly heated. Stir in cilantro, basil, and lime juice. Ladle soup into each of 8 bowls; top evenly with Sriracha. Serve with lime wedges.

SERVING SIZE: 1¼ cups soup, 1 teaspoon Sriracha, and 1 lime wedge

CALORIES 231; FAT 8.7g (sat 3.8g, mono 0g, poly 0.1g); PROTEIN 11g; CARB 27g; FIBER 2g; SUGARS 3g (est. added sugars 1g); CHOL 71mg; IRON 1mg; SODIUM 390mg; CALC 50mg

ALMOND-CRUSTED TILAPIA
WITH LEMON-CAPER SAUCE

You can usually find a variety of nut- and spice-crusted tilapia at the fish counter of your local supermarket. Pair it with a quick lemon-caper pan sauce and already roasted or grilled green beans from the deli counter, and you'll have dinner on the table in less than half an hour.

SERVES 4 • HANDS-ON TIME: 14 MIN. • TOTAL TIME: 23 MIN.

4   (6-ounce) almond-crusted tilapia fillets (such as Fresh Market)
Cooking spray
2   cups pregrilled green beans with red and yellow bell peppers (such as Whole Foods)
½   cup roasted tomatoes, coarsely chopped
3   tablespoons coarsely chopped pitted kalamata olives
2   teaspoons balsamic vinegar
⅛   teaspoon freshly ground black pepper
2   tablespoons unsalted butter
1   tablespoon olive oil
½   teaspoon grated lemon rind
3   tablespoons chopped fresh parsley
2   tablespoons fresh lemon juice
1   tablespoon capers, drained
¼   teaspoon salt
4   lemon slices

1 Preheat oven to 400°F.

2 Heat a large nonstick skillet over medium-high heat. Coat fish with cooking spray; cook fish, in 2 batches, 2 minutes on each side or until lightly browned. Transfer to a foil-lined baking sheet. Bake at 400°F for 10 minutes or until fish flakes easily when tested with a fork. Keep warm.

3 While fish bakes, combine grilled green beans and next 4 ingredients (through pepper) in a large bowl; toss well. Transfer to a metal baking pan lightly coated with cooking spray. Bake, uncovered, at 400°F for 8 minutes or until thoroughly heated.

4 Wipe drippings from skillet with a paper towel; add butter and olive oil, and cook over medium heat 2 minutes or until butter melts and begins to foam. Stir in lemon rind and next 4 ingredients (through salt). Serve fish with lemon-caper sauce, roasted green bean mixture, and lemon slices.

SERVING SIZE: 1 fish fillet, 1 tablespoon sauce, ⅔ cup green bean mixture, and 1 lemon slice

CALORIES 512; FAT 35.9g (sat 6.9g, mono 16.4g, poly 5.5g); PROTEIN 32g; CARB 20g; FIBER 6g; SUGARS 7g (est. added sugars 6g); CHOL 70mg; IRON 0mg; SODIUM 569mg; CALC 11mg

Eat Now & Later

Make a simple salad with your leftover tilapia. Break up the fish, and toss it with spinach and Cilantro-Chile Vinaigrette (page 269).

SEARED SALMON
WITH ROASTED GRAPE TOMATOES

Roasting the grape tomatoes brings out their sweetness, making them a great complement for this flaky fish.

SERVES 4 • HANDS-ON TIME: 11 MIN. • TOTAL TIME: 19 MIN.

2   cups multicolored grape tomatoes
Cooking spray
5   teaspoons olive oil, divided
1   (1½-pound) salmon fillet, cut crosswise into 4 equal pieces
½   teaspoon kosher salt, divided
¼   teaspoon freshly ground black pepper, divided
½   teaspoon grated lemon rind

2   teaspoons fresh lemon juice
2   teaspoons rice vinegar
½   teaspoon Dijon mustard
½   teaspoon honey
4   cups Mediterranean kale salad (such as Whole Foods)
1   teaspoon thyme leaves
4 lemon wedges

❶ Preheat oven to 400°F.

❷ Place grape tomatoes on a metal baking sheet lightly coated with cooking spray. Lightly coat tomatoes with cooking spray. Bake at 400°F for 12 minutes or until lightly browned and beginning to caramelize.

❸ While tomatoes bake, heat a large ovenproof nonstick skillet over medium-high heat until hot. Add 2 teaspoons oil; swirl to coat. Sprinkle salmon with ¼ teaspoon kosher salt and ⅛ teaspoon pepper. Lightly coat salmon with cooking spray; place salmon, skin side up, in pan. Cook 3 minutes or until golden brown. Turn salmon over. Place skillet in oven. Bake at 400°F for 6 minutes or until fish flakes easily when tested with a fork. Keep warm.

❹ Combine remaining 1 tablespoon olive oil, lemon rind, and next 4 ingredients (through honey) in a small bowl; stir well with a whisk. Drizzle dressing over kale salad; toss well. Combine roasted tomatoes, thyme leaves, remaining ¼ teaspoon salt, and remaining ⅛ teaspoon pepper, pressing tomatoes gently with the back of a fork to release juices; toss well. Top salmon with roasted tomato mixture, and serve with kale salad and lemon wedges.

SERVING SIZE: 1 fish fillet, ⅓ cup roasted tomatoes, 1 cup kale salad, and 1 lemon wedge

CALORIES 376; **FAT** 16g (sat 2.2g, mono 7.9g, poly 2.4g); **PROTEIN** 39g; **CARB** 18g; **FIBER** 4g; **SUGARS** 7g (est. added sugars 3g); **CHOL** 78mg; **IRON** 8mg; **SODIUM** 506mg; **CALC** 14mg

FISH TACOS
WITH CILANTRO-AVOCADO SLAW

Pick up seasoned fish chunks or fillets at the seafood department of your local supermarket for these quick grilled fish tacos. For an extra hit of smokiness, sprinkle fish with a blend of ancho chile powder and ground cumin.

SERVES 4 • HANDS-ON TIME: 20 MIN. • TOTAL TIME: 20 MIN.

2   cups bagged cabbage-and-carrot coleslaw

⅓   cup cilantro-avocado yogurt dressing (such as Bolthouse Farms)

2   tablespoons fresh lime juice, divided

2   cups prepared grilled corn-and-onion salad (such as Whole Foods)

1   cup rinsed and drained canned black beans

¼   cup chopped fresh cilantro

2   tablespoons minced seeded jalapeño pepper (1 small pepper)

Cooking spray

1   pound chipotle-lime-seasoned firm white fish chunks (such as Whole Foods)

8   (6-inch) corn tortillas

8   lime wedges

1 Combine coleslaw, yogurt dressing, and 1 tablespoon lime juice; toss gently to coat.

2 Combine remaining 1 tablespoon lime juice, corn salad, and next 3 ingredients (through jalapeño); toss well.

3 Heat a grill pan over medium-high heat. Coat grill pan with cooking spray. Add fish to pan; grill 2 to 3 minutes on each side or until fish flakes easily when tested with a fork. Remove fish from pan.

4 Lightly coat tortillas with cooking spray. Grill 1 minute on each side or until lightly browned. Place 1½ ounces fish and ¼ cup slaw in center of each tortilla; fold in half. Serve with corn–black bean salad and lime wedges.

SERVING SIZE: 2 tacos, ¾ cup salad, and 2 lime wedges

CALORIES 416; FAT 9.8g (sat 0.8g, mono 2.2g, poly 2.1g); PROTEIN 30g; CARB 55g; FIBER 11g; SUGARS 7g (est. added sugars 5g); CHOL 43mg; IRON 1mg; SODIUM 767mg; CALC 49mg

RED CURRY SHRIMP SAUTÉ
WITH JASMINE RICE

Leave the soy sauce on the shelf, and use red curry paste to add some spark to the traditional shrimp-and-rice combination.

SERVES 4 • HANDS-ON TIME: 20 MIN. • TOTAL TIME: 23 MIN.

1½ cups water
1 cup uncooked jasmine rice
2 teaspoons canola oil
1 cup thinly vertically sliced onion
1 cup thinly sliced red bell pepper
1½ tablespoons red curry paste
1 cup light coconut milk

¾ pound peeled and deveined large shrimp
2 teaspoons fresh lime juice
1 teaspoon fish sauce
Torn cilantro leaves (optional)
4 lime wedges

1 Bring 1½ cups water to a boil in a medium saucepan; stir in rice. Cover, reduce heat, and simmer 18 minutes or until liquid is absorbed. Remove from heat. Let stand 5 minutes; fluff with a fork.

2 While rice cooks, heat a large nonstick skillet over medium-high heat. Add oil to pan; swirl to coat. Add onion and bell pepper; sauté 6 minutes or until tender and beginning to brown. Add curry paste; sauté 1 minute. Stir in coconut milk; bring to a simmer. Add shrimp; cook, stirring frequently, 3 minutes or until shrimp are done. Remove from heat; stir in lime juice and fish sauce.

3 Place rice into each of 4 bowls. Spoon shrimp mixture evenly over rice; top with cilantro, if desired. Serve with lime wedges.

SERVING SIZE: ¾ cup rice, ¾ cup shrimp mixture, and 1 lime wedge

CALORIES 306; FAT 7.3g (sat 3.9g, mono 1.6g, poly 0.9g); PROTEIN 15g; CARB 42g; FIBER 1g; SUGARS 3g (est. added sugars 0g); CHOL 107mg; IRON 2mg; SODIUM 758mg; CALC 63mg

Savvy Shortcuts

Peeling and deveining shrimp can be time-consuming. Ask at the grocery store fish counter if they offer that service for free, or spend a little extra cash on cook-ready shrimp.

MUSHROOM RAVIOLI AND WINTER VEGETABLES
IN BUTTERNUT BROTH

Pasta and soup pair up for a simple dinner full of exquisite flavors. Adding butternut soup to the vegetable broth is an easy way to create complexity.

SERVES 4 • HANDS-ON TIME: 24 MIN. • TOTAL TIME: 24 MIN.

2　cups lower-sodium vegetable broth (such as Pacific)

½　cup lower-sodium creamy butternut squash soup (such as Pacific)

¼　cup dry white wine

2　teaspoons refrigerated Italian herb paste (such as Gourmet Garden)

1　teaspoon olive oil

1　(8-ounce) package presliced cremini mushrooms

¼　teaspoon salt

¼　teaspoon coarsely ground black pepper

1　(8-ounce) package refrigerated butternut squash chunks (1¾ cups)

1　(8-ounce) package frozen wild chanterelle mushroom ravioli

3　cups loosely packed baby kale

1　ounce fresh Parmesan cheese, finely shaved (about ¼ cup)

Fried sage leaves (optional)

1 Combine first 4 ingredients in a large saucepan. Bring to a boil; reduce heat, and simmer, uncovered, 10 minutes.

2 While broth mixture cooks, heat a large nonstick skillet over medium-high heat. Add olive oil; swirl to coat. Add mushrooms, salt, and pepper. Cook, stirring frequently, 6 minutes or until liquid evaporates and mushrooms are golden brown. Add butternut squash; sauté 4 minutes. Add broth mixture and ravioli. Cover and reduce heat to medium. Cook 8 minutes or until pasta is tender.

3 Add kale, stirring until wilted. Ladle soup into each of 4 bowls; top evenly with cheese. Garnish with fried sage leaves, if desired. Serve immediately.

SERVING SIZE: 1 cup broth mixture and 1 tablespoon cheese

CALORIES 259; FAT 5g (sat 2.2g, mono 1.4g, poly 0.3g); PROTEIN 11g; CARB 40g; FIBER 5g; SUGARS 5g (est. added sugars 0g); CHOL 14mg; IRON 6mg; SODIUM 650mg; CALC 222mg

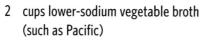

Eat Now & Later

Turn that leftover **butternut squash soup** into soup shooters—a party-ready appetizer—or reduce it in a pan over medium heat, add some half-and-half and sage, and make it into a personality-packed sauce for pasta and protein.

MEATLESS "CHICKEN" TINGA GYROS

Curb your Greek and Mexican cravings in one meatless mash-up of a torta and classic gyro sandwich.

SERVES 6 • HANDS-ON TIME: 23 MIN. • TOTAL TIME: 23 MIN.

1   (10.6-ounce) package frozen smoky chipotle tinga-flavored meatless chicken (such as Sol Cuisine)

Cooking spray

6   (8-inch) pitas (such as Toufayan)

1   (16-ounce) package refrigerated presliced bell pepper and onion for fajitas, coarsely chopped (4 cups)

1   teaspoon fresh lime juice

¼   teaspoon kosher salt

¼   teaspoon ground cumin

½   cup premade guacamole (such as Whole Foods)

¼   cup low-fat sour cream

2   tablespoons fresh lime juice

3   cups shredded iceberg lettuce

❶ Combine all ingredients from package of meatless chicken in a medium microwave-safe bowl. Microwave, uncovered, at HIGH 3 minutes; stir. Microwave an additional 3 minutes or until hot. Cover and keep warm.

❷ Preheat a large heavy grill pan over medium-high heat.

❸ Coat grill pan with cooking spray. Coat both sides of pitas with cooking spray, and place in grill pan. Cook 30 seconds on each side or until grill marks appear. Wrap pitas in foil, and keep warm.

❹ Add chopped vegetables to pan. Coat vegetables with cooking spray; sprinkle with 1 teaspoon lime juice, salt, and ¼ teaspoon cumin. Cook 5 minutes or until vegetables are slightly softened and beginning to brown, stirring occasionally. Stir vegetables into cooked meatless chicken mixture; cover and keep warm.

❺ Combine guacamole, sour cream, and 2 tablespoons lime juice in a small bowl, stirring until smooth.

❻ Spoon ⅔ cup vegetable mixture down center of each pita. Top each with 2 tablespoons guacamole mixture and ½ cup lettuce; roll up. Serve immediately.

SERVING SIZE: 1 gyro

CALORIES 299; FAT 7.8g (sat 1.4g, mono 3.6g, poly 0.9g); PROTEIN 15g; CARB 45g; FIBER 6g; SUGARS 8g (est. added sugars 3g); CHOL 4mg; IRON 5mg; SODIUM 542mg; CALC 101mg

Seasonal Switch-Up

Get creative with your vegetables according to the season: Try a mix of shredded Napa cabbage, sliced radishes, thinly sliced red onions, and even arugula for added flavor.

CHAPTER 2

EXPEDITED ENTRÉES

....

Your supermarket's olive bar is there for a reason—and we'd like to think it's to help make life a lot easier. That's because those roasted tomatoes and garlic make a mean marinara; cipollini onions, Peppadew peppers, and bright green Castelvetrano olives create briny chutney for seared snapper; and kalamatas add bite to eggs poached in spicy sauce. In this chapter, we look at more ways to use grocery store goodies—think frozen foods, precut fruits and veggies, and deli items—to save time and make dinners *A.S.A.P.*, and, of course, more delicious.

CHICKEN FRIED RICE
WITH EDAMAME

Packed with three kinds of protein—chicken, edamame, and eggs—this quick and easy dish fills everyone up without weighing them down.

SERVES 4 • HANDS-ON TIME: 20 MIN. • TOTAL TIME: 20 MIN.

Savvy Shortcuts

Gotta get out the door A.S.A.P.? Save even more time using precooked chicken breasts and brown rice.

2 tablespoons canola oil, divided
½ pound chicken tenderloins, cut into bite-sized pieces
¼ teaspoon salt
1 cup frozen shelled edamame (green soybeans)
2 tablespoons water
½ cup thinly sliced green onions (3 medium)

2 teaspoons minced peeled fresh ginger
2 garlic cloves, minced
2 cups cooked brown rice, chilled
2 large eggs, beaten
2 tablespoons lower-sodium soy sauce
1 teaspoon dark sesame oil

1 Heat a large nonstick skillet over medium-high heat. Add 1 tablespoon canola oil to pan; swirl to coat. Sprinkle chicken with salt. Add chicken to pan; sauté 5 minutes. Transfer chicken to a medium bowl. Add edamame and 2 tablespoons water to pan; cook, stirring constantly, 2 to 3 minutes or just until tender. Add edamame to chicken.

2 Wipe pan dry with a paper towel. Add remaining 1 tablespoon canola oil to pan; swirl to coat. Add green onions, ginger, and garlic; cook, stirring constantly, 15 seconds. Add brown rice, stirring until coated with oil. Cook rice mixture, without stirring, 2 minutes or until edges begin to brown. Stir; flatten rice mixture to an even thickness with the back of a spoon. Cook, without stirring, 2 minutes.

3 Push rice mixture to edges of pan using a wooden spoon to create a well in center; add beaten eggs to well. Cook 20 seconds or until eggs begin to set. Stir gently to scramble eggs. Cook 30 seconds, stirring constantly to blend egg into rice mixture.

4 Stir in chicken mixture, soy sauce, and sesame oil. Serve immediately.

SERVING SIZE: 1 cup

CALORIES 340; FAT 14.8g (sat 2.2g, mono 6.6g, poly 3.5g); PROTEIN 23g; CARB 28g; FIBER 3g; SUGARS 2g (est. added sugars 0g); CHOL 134mg; IRON 2mg; SODIUM 503mg; CALC 67mg

CHIPOTLE-SPIKED CHICKEN FAJITAS

Heat up the midweek menu with tender chicken fajitas in a chipotle chile–spiked marinade. Serve with an assortment of fresh pico de gallo, sliced red Fresno chile, and cilantro sprigs.

SERVES 4 • HANDS-ON TIME: 24 MIN. • TOTAL TIME: 54 MIN., INCLUDING MARINATE TIME

⅔ cup Mexican beer
2 tablespoons lower-sodium soy sauce
2 tablespoons fresh lime juice
1½ tablespoons chopped chipotle chile, canned in adobo sauce
1 tablespoon canola oil
¾ teaspoon chili powder
½ teaspoon ground cumin
¼ teaspoon smoked paprika
2 garlic cloves, crushed

1 pound skinless, boneless chicken breast halves, cut into ½-inch strips
2 (6.5-ounce) packages refrigerated presliced fajita vegetables
Cooking spray
8 (6-inch) 96%-fat-free flour tortillas (such as Mission)
¼ cup light sour cream
8 lime wedges

① Place first 9 ingredients in a blender or food processor; process until smooth. Divide mixture evenly between 2 large heavy-duty zip-top plastic bags. Add chicken to 1 bag; seal bag, and marinate at room temperature 30 minutes, turning occasionally. Repeat procedure with vegetables and marinade in remaining bag. Remove chicken and vegetables from bags; discard marinade.

② Preheat a grill pan over medium-high heat.

③ Coat grill pan with cooking spray. Grill chicken and vegetables, in batches, 6 minutes or until chicken is done and vegetables are crisp-tender, turning frequently.

④ While chicken and vegetables cook, warm tortillas according to package directions. Place 1½ ounces grilled chicken into each tortilla, and top evenly with vegetable mixture; fold up. Serve with light sour cream and lime wedges.

SERVING SIZE: 2 fajitas, 1 tablespoon sour cream, and 2 lime wedges

CALORIES 395; FAT 8.6g (sat 1.8g, mono 2.4g, poly 1.1g); PROTEIN 31g; CARB 43g; FIBER 6g; SUGARS 6g (est. added sugars 2g); CHOL 88mg; IRON 1mg; SODIUM 634mg; CALC 44mg

Eat Now & Later

A little leftover beer goes a long way. Use it to braise beef, turn your Bloody Mary into a michelada, or drop in a scoop of vanilla ice cream to make a beer float.

MEDITERRANEAN CHICKEN ROULADE

No need for a side vegetable with these tasty bundles of chicken—asparagus and roasted bell peppers bake right inside. Make them assembly-line style in minutes, and then pop them in the oven while you prepare a grain-based side to round out the meal.

SERVES 4 • HANDS-ON TIME: 10 MIN. • TOTAL TIME: 30 MIN.

4   chicken cutlets (1¼ pounds)
2   tablespoons refrigerated reduced-fat pesto
1   ounce crumbled feta cheese (about ¼ cup)
16   roasted asparagus spears (such as Whole Foods deli)

3   ounces drained bottled roasted red bell peppers, cut into 8 strips
Cooking spray
½   teaspoon freshly ground black pepper
¼   teaspoon kosher salt
¼   cup panko (Japanese breadcrumbs)

1 Preheat oven to 375°F.

2 Place chicken cutlets between 2 sheets of plastic wrap; pound to ½-inch thickness using a meat mallet or small heavy skillet. Spread 1½ teaspoons pesto over each cutlet. Sprinkle each with 1 tablespoon cheese.

3 Place 4 asparagus spears parallel to long side of 1 cutlet. Place 2 red bell pepper strips lengthwise on top of asparagus. Tightly roll up cutlet into a bundle; secure with wooden picks. Place bundle on a baking sheet coated with cooking spray. Repeat procedure with remaining asparagus, cutlets, and bell pepper strips.

4 Coat bundles with cooking spray, and sprinkle evenly with pepper and salt.

5 Bake at 375°F for 20 minutes. Let stand 2 minutes.

6 While bundles cook, place panko in a small nonstick skillet; coat panko with cooking spray. Cook, stirring often, over medium-high heat 1 minute or until golden. Remove wooden picks from bundles, and cut crosswise into slices. Sprinkle bundles evenly with panko.

SERVING SIZE: 1 bundle and 1 tablespoon panko

CALORIES 275; FAT 9.8g (sat 2.9g, mono 2.6g, poly 1g); PROTEIN 36g; CARB 10g; FIBER 2g; SUGARS 3g (est. added sugars 0g); CHOL 114mg; IRON 2mg; SODIUM 465mg; CALC 95mg

Eat Now & Later

Top cold noodles with leftover roulade slices, and drizzle with olive oil for a filling lunch pasta salad.

WEEKNIGHT LEMON CHICKEN SKILLET DINNER

It doesn't get much easier, or more satisfying: a complete dinner in one pan in half an hour. The lemon brightens this cozy meal.

SERVES 4 • HANDS-ON TIME: 30 MIN. • TOTAL TIME: 30 MIN.

12 ounces baby red potatoes, halved
1 tablespoon olive oil, divided
4 (6-ounce) skinless, boneless chicken breast halves, pounded to ¾-inch thickness
¾ teaspoon kosher salt, divided
½ teaspoon freshly ground black pepper, divided
2 thyme sprigs
4 ounces cremini mushrooms, quartered

1 tablespoon chopped fresh thyme
¼ cup whole milk
5 teaspoons all-purpose flour
1¾ cups unsalted chicken stock (such as Swanson)
8 very thin lemon slices
1 (8-ounce) package trimmed haricots verts (French green beans)
2 tablespoons chopped fresh flat-leaf parsley

1 Preheat oven to 450°F.

2 Place potatoes in a medium saucepan; cover with water. Bring to a boil, and simmer 12 minutes or until tender. Drain.

3 Heat a large ovenproof skillet over medium-high heat. Add 1 teaspoon oil to pan; swirl to coat. Sprinkle chicken with ¼ teaspoon salt and ¼ teaspoon pepper. Add chicken and thyme sprigs to pan; cook 5 minutes or until chicken is browned. Turn chicken over. Place pan in oven; bake at 450°F for 10 minutes or until chicken is done. Remove chicken from pan.

4 Return pan to medium-high heat. Add remaining 2 teaspoons oil to pan; swirl to coat. Add potatoes, cut sides down; mushrooms; and 1 tablespoon thyme; cook 3 minutes or until browned, stirring once. Combine milk and flour in a small bowl, stirring with a whisk. Add remaining salt, remaining pepper, flour mixture, stock, lemon, and beans to pan; simmer 1 minute or until slightly thickened. Add chicken; cover, reduce heat, and simmer 3 minutes or until beans are crisp-tender. Sprinkle with parsley.

SERVING SIZE: 1 chicken breast half and ¾ cup potato mixture

CALORIES 342; FAT 8.6g (sat 1.8g, mono 3.9g, poly 1.2g); PROTEIN 43g; CARB 23g; FIBER 4g; SUGARS 4g (est. added sugars 0g); CHOL 110mg; IRON 3mg; SODIUM 642mg; CALC 77mg

ROASTED TOMATO-CHEESE STUFFED CHICKEN BREASTS

That's the stuff! Chicken breasts filled with roasted tomatoes and herbed cheese make for a quick, elegant entrée. Pair with rice pilaf or oven-roasted potatoes and a simple salad.

SERVES 4 • HANDS-ON TIME: 23 MIN. • TOTAL TIME: 28 MIN.

4 (6-ounce) skinless, boneless chicken breast halves
½ cup roasted tomatoes (about 3½ ounces; such as Whole Foods olive bar)
½ cup light buttery garlic-and-herb spreadable cheese (such as Boursin)

3 teaspoons olive oil, divided
½ teaspoon kosher salt
¼ teaspoon freshly ground black pepper
Cooking spray
¼ cup chopped fresh parsley
1½ teaspoons grated lemon rind

1 Preheat oven to 400°F.

2 Place each chicken breast half between 2 sheets of heavy-duty plastic wrap; pound to ¾-inch thickness using a meat mallet or small heavy skillet. Cut a horizontal slit through thickest portion of each chicken breast half to form a pocket. Stuff 2 tablespoons roasted tomatoes and 2 tablespoons cheese into each pocket; close opening with a wooden pick.

3 Heat a large nonstick ovenproof skillet over medium-high heat. Add 2 teaspoons olive oil; swirl to coat. Sprinkle chicken with salt and pepper. Lightly coat chicken with cooking spray; cook 2 minutes or until golden brown. Turn chicken over; place pan in oven. Bake at 400°F for 14 minutes or until done. Remove from oven; let stand 5 minutes.

4 Combine parsley, lemon rind, and remaining 1 teaspoon olive oil; stir well. Top chicken with parsley mixture.

SERVING SIZE: 1 stuffed chicken breast half and 1 tablespoon parsley mixture

CALORIES 325; **FAT** 15g (sat 4g, mono 4.1g, poly 1.3g); **PROTEIN** 40g; **CARB** 4g; **FIBER** 1g; **SUGARS** 3g (est. added sugars 0g); **CHOL** 134mg; **IRON** 1mg; **SODIUM** 583mg; **CALC** 35mg

CHICKEN WRAPS
WITH JICAMA-PINEAPPLE SLAW

Flatbread isn't just for pizzas: Use it as a wrap for this island-inspired combination of rotisserie chicken and fast, fruity slaw.

SERVES 4 • HANDS-ON TIME: 10 MIN. • TOTAL TIME: 10 MIN.

¼ cup reduced-fat mayonnaise
1½ tablespoons rice vinegar
½ teaspoon honey
¼ teaspoon salt
⅛ teaspoon freshly ground black pepper
2 cups bagged cabbage-and-carrot coleslaw
½ cup chopped fresh pineapple
½ cup (1½-inch) julienne-cut peeled jicama
⅓ cup sliced green onions
3 tablespoons chopped fresh cilantro
1⅓ cups shredded rotisserie chicken
4 (1.86-ounce) light original-flavor flatbreads (such as Flatout)

Eat Now & Later

Jicama, also called yam bean or Mexican turnip, is an edible root with a water chestnut-like texture and flavor. Use the leftovers in salsa or to add some crunch to potato salad.

1 Combine first 5 ingredients in a large bowl, stirring with a whisk. Add coleslaw and next 4 ingredients (through cilantro); toss to coat.

2 Place ⅓ cup chicken and ½ cup slaw mixture along 1 short side of each flatbread; roll up. Cut wraps diagonally in half, if desired.

SERVING SIZE: 1 wrap

CALORIES 220; FAT 8.6g (sat 1.2g, mono 2g, poly 2.4g); PROTEIN 20g; CARB 24g; FIBER 11g; SUGARS 5g (est. added sugars 1g); CHOL 44mg; IRON 2mg; SODIUM 617mg; CALC 45mg

SPICED CHICKEN AND APRICOT SKEWERS

Chicken again? Not quite. Blow guests away with the incredible taste that comes from the unlikely pairing of apricot preserves and chile paste. A bed of white rice is the perfect accompaniment.

SERVES 4 • HANDS-ON TIME: 24 MIN. • TOTAL TIME: 3 HR. 39 MIN., INCLUDING MARINATE TIME

⅓ cup apricot preserves
¼ cup rice vinegar
3 tablespoons lower-sodium soy sauce
2 tablespoons canola oil
1 tablespoon chile paste with garlic (such as sambal oelek)
1 teaspoon ground coriander
¼ teaspoon crushed red pepper

1 pound skinless, boneless chicken thighs (about 3), cut into 1½-inch pieces
1 cup boiling water
12 dried apricots (about ½ cup)
½ large red onion, cut into 1½-inch pieces
Cooking spray
Cilantro sprigs

① Place first 7 ingredients in a blender or food processor; process until smooth. Pour marinade into a large heavy-duty zip-top plastic bag. Add chicken; seal bag, and marinate in refrigerator 3 hours, turning bag occasionally. Remove chicken from bag, reserving marinade.

② Combine boiling water and apricots in a bowl. Cover and let stand 15 minutes. Drain.

③ Bring reserved marinade to a boil in a small saucepan over medium-high heat; boil 2 minutes. Remove from heat; cool 10 minutes or until room temperature.

④ Preheat grill to medium-high heat.

⑤ Thread chicken, apricots, and red onion alternately onto 4 (10-inch) metal skewers. Place kebabs on grill rack coated with cooking spray; grill 12 minutes or until a thermometer registers 165°F, turning kebabs occasionally and brushing frequently with marinade after 6 minutes. Sprinkle with cilantro.

SERVING SIZE: 1 skewer

CALORIES 274; FAT 10.3g (sat 1.7g, mono 5.2g, poly 2.6g); PROTEIN 24g; CARB 22g; FIBER 1g; SUGARS 15g (est. added sugars 5g); CHOL 107mg; IRON 1mg; SODIUM 503mg; CALC 24mg

TANDOORI CHICKEN PIZZA

Indian-inspired pizza topped with a cool cucumber salad gives pizza night an exotic upgrade.

SERVES 4 • HANDS-ON TIME: 15 MIN. • TOTAL TIME: 25 MIN.

2 (3-ounce) naan breads
2 teaspoons olive oil, divided
1½ teaspoons salt-free tandoori masala seasoning, divided (such as Savory Spice Shop)
4 ounces rotisserie chicken breast, pulled into large shreds (1 cup)
½ cup thin vertical red onion slices
2 ounces queso fresco, shredded

2 tablespoons plain fat-free Greek yogurt
1 tablespoon tahini (roasted sesame seed paste)
1 teaspoon water
⅛ teaspoon salt
2 teaspoons fresh lemon juice, divided
1 cup thin English cucumber slices, halved (½ medium)
1 cup packed baby arugula

❶ Preheat oven to 425°F.

❷ Cover a large baking sheet with parchment paper; place naan on baking sheet. Brush each naan with ½ teaspoon olive oil, and sprinkle each with ½ teaspoon masala seasoning.

❸ Combine chicken, ½ teaspoon olive oil, and remaining ½ teaspoon masala seasoning. Top each naan with ½ cup chicken mixture and ¼ cup onion; sprinkle each with ¼ cup cheese. Bake at 425°F for 15 minutes or until edges of naan are golden and crisp and toppings are thoroughly heated.

❹ Combine yogurt, tahini, 1 teaspoon water, salt, and 1½ teaspoons lemon juice in a medium bowl, stirring with a whisk. Add cucumber, tossing to coat.

❺ Combine arugula, remaining ½ teaspoon lemon juice, and remaining ½ teaspoon olive oil, tossing to coat.

❻ Top each pizza with ½ cup cucumber mixture and ½ cup arugula mixture. Serve immediately.

SERVING SIZE: ½ pizza

CALORIES 277; FAT 13.2g (sat 3.7g, mono 3.6g, poly 1.4g); PROTEIN 16g; CARB 25g; FIBER 2g; SUGARS 4g (est. added sugars 1g); CHOL 37mg; IRON 1mg; SODIUM 563mg; CALC 112mg

PEPPER JELLY-GLAZED CHICKEN

The perennial party appetizer of pepper jelly and cream cheese packs this chicken dish with sweet heat. Use green, red, or a little of both.

SERVES 4 • HANDS-ON TIME: 15 MIN. • TOTAL TIME: 25 MIN.

¼ cup ⅓-less-fat cream cheese, softened
2 teaspoons chopped fresh cilantro
4 (6-ounce) skinless, boneless chicken breast halves
¼ teaspoon salt
½ cup hot pepper jelly (such as Stonewall Kitchen Hot Pepper Jelly)
2 tablespoons fresh lime juice
Cooking spray

1 Preheat grill to medium-high heat.

2 Combine cream cheese and cilantro in a small bowl, stirring until blended.

3 Cut a 2½-inch horizontal slit through thickest portion of each chicken breast half to form a pocket. Stuff about 1 tablespoon cheese mixture into each pocket; secure with wooden picks. Sprinkle chicken evenly with salt.

4 Combine pepper jelly and lime juice in a small bowl; divide mixture in half. Place chicken on grill rack coated with cooking spray; grill 7 to 8 minutes. Turn chicken over; brush with half of jelly mixture. Grill 7 to 8 minutes or until a thermometer registers 165°F, brushing with remaining half of jelly mixture during last 2 minutes of cooking time.

SERVING SIZE: 1 chicken breast half

CALORIES 322; FAT 7.7g (sat 2.8g, mono 2g, poly 0.9g); PROTEIN 40g; CARB 21g; FIBER 0g; SUGARS 21g (est. added sugars 17g); CHOL 135mg; IRON 1mg; SODIUM 269mg; CALC 26mg

COCONUT-CRUSTED CHICKEN TENDERS

These oven-baked tenders get a slight sweetness from the coconut, making them very kid-friendly. When feeding the family, use regular mango chutney instead of hot.

SERVES 4 • HANDS-ON TIME: 8 MIN. • TOTAL TIME: 24 MIN.

Cooking spray
¼ cup all-purpose flour
1 large egg, lightly beaten
1 tablespoon water
⅓ cup finely shredded
   unsweetened coconut
⅓ cup panko (Japanese breadcrumbs)

1 pound chicken breast tenders
   (8 tenders)
¼ teaspoon salt
¼ teaspoon freshly ground black pepper
¼ cup hot mango chutney
1½ teaspoons rice vinegar
1 teaspoon Dijon mustard

1 Preheat oven to 450°F.

2 Set a rack coated with cooking spray over a foil-lined rimmed baking sheet.

3 Lightly spoon flour into a dry measuring cup; level with a knife. Place flour in a shallow dish. Combine egg and 1 tablespoon water in another shallow dish. Combine coconut and panko in a third shallow dish.

4 Sprinkle chicken tenders with salt and pepper. Dredge chicken tenders in flour; dip in egg mixture. Dredge in coconut mixture, pressing to adhere. Coat chicken tenders with cooking spray; place on rack. Bake at 450°F for 8 minutes. Turn chicken over; bake an additional 8 minutes or until golden brown and done.

5 Combine chutney, rice vinegar, and mustard in a small bowl. Serve chicken with chutney.

SERVING SIZE: 2 chicken tenders and 1 tablespoon chutney mixture

CALORIES 277; FAT 8.1g (sat 4.2g, mono 1.4g, poly 0.8g); PROTEIN 28g; CARB 21g; FIBER 1g; SUGARS 14g (est. added sugars 5g); CHOL 125mg; IRON 1mg; SODIUM 562mg; CALC 13mg

Eat Now & Later

Warm up a pita or wrap, fill it with chopped-up leftover chicken, top with mango chutney, and make a lunch of it. Add a few chips to balance out the sweetness.

ROASTED TURKEY TENDERLOINS
WITH HERB-MUSHROOM SAUCE

Gravy tends to mask the delicate flavors of turkey, but this savory sauce is celebrated for its subtlety. It's also a simple sauce to whip up when serving all those post-Thanksgiving leftovers.

SERVES 6 • HANDS-ON TIME: 25 MIN. • TOTAL TIME: 35 MIN.

1   (1½-pound) package turkey tenderloins
1½ tablespoons salt-free garlic-and-herb seasoning (such as Mrs. Dash)
1   tablespoon canola oil
¼   cup chopped shallots (1 medium)
½   teaspoon freshly ground black pepper
¼   teaspoon kosher salt
1   (8-ounce) package presliced cremini mushrooms
1   tablespoon sherry vinegar
1   tablespoon Dijon mustard
1   teaspoon honey
1   cup fat-free, lower-sodium chicken broth (such as Swanson)
1   tablespoon chopped fresh tarragon
1   tablespoon chopped fresh chives
2   teaspoons butter

1 Preheat oven to 400°F.

2 Rub surface of turkey with salt-free seasoning. Heat a large nonstick skillet over medium-high heat. Add oil to pan; swirl to coat. Cook turkey 2 minutes on each side or until browned. Remove pan from heat. Transfer turkey to a foil-lined rimmed baking sheet.

3 Bake at 400°F for 26 minutes or until a thermometer registers 165°F. Let stand 5 minutes.

4 Return skillet to medium-high heat. Add shallots and next 3 ingredients (through mushrooms) to pan. Cook, stirring frequently, 6 minutes or until liquid evaporates and mushrooms are golden brown.

5 Stir in vinegar, mustard, and honey; cook 30 seconds, stirring constantly. Stir in chicken broth, scraping pan to loosen browned bits. Stir in tarragon and chives; reduce heat, and simmer, uncovered, 10 minutes or until sauce thickens slightly. Add butter, stirring until melted. Cut turkey into slices, and drizzle with sauce.

SERVING SIZE: 3 ounces turkey and 2 tablespoons sauce

CALORIES 176; FAT 5.2g (sat 1g, mono 2.1g, poly 1g); PROTEIN 29g; CARB 5g; FIBER 1g; SUGARS 3g (est. added sugars 1g); CHOL 48mg; IRON 2mg; SODIUM 313mg; CALC 14mg

Eat Now & Later

Leftover turkey and sauce? Cooked quinoa or couscous from the supermarket deli or salad bar makes a fun foundation for a cold lunch salad. Bonus points—and flavor—if it's studded with cranberries.

CUBAN-STYLE SKIRT STEAK WITH MOJO

Mojo, a signature sauce in Cuban cuisine, is traditionally made with Seville oranges, which are quite sour. Our recipe uses a combination of navel orange, lime, and lemon juices to replicate the tartness of the traditional.

SERVES 6 • HANDS-ON TIME: 14 MIN. • TOTAL TIME: 4 HR. 19 MIN., INCLUDING MARINATE TIME

¼ cup fresh navel orange juice
¼ cup extra-virgin olive oil
2 tablespoons fresh lime juice
2 tablespoons fresh lemon juice
2 teaspoons chopped fresh oregano
1 teaspoon ground cumin
1 teaspoon kosher salt, divided
¼ teaspoon freshly ground black pepper
6 large garlic cloves
1 (1½-pound) skirt steak, trimmed
Cooking spray
Parsley leaves (optional)

1 Place first 6 ingredients, ¾ teaspoon salt, pepper, and garlic in a blender; process 30 seconds or until smooth. Reserve ¼ cup marinade. Place remaining ¾ cup marinade in a large heavy-duty zip-top plastic bag. Add steak to bag; seal bag, and marinate in refrigerator 4 hours, turning bag occasionally. Remove steak from bag; discard marinade.

2 Preheat grill to medium-high heat.

3 Sprinkle steak with remaining ¼ teaspoon salt. Place steak on grill rack coated with cooking spray; grill 6 minutes or until desired degree of doneness, turning once. Let stand 5 minutes. Cut steak diagonally across grain into thin slices. Arrange steak slices on a platter, and drizzle with reserved ¼ cup marinade. Sprinkle with parsley, if desired.

SERVING SIZE: 3 ounces steak and 2 teaspoons mojo
CALORIES 256; **FAT** 17.1g (sat 4.7g, mono 9.5g, poly 1.5g); **PROTEIN** 24g; **CARB** 2g; **FIBER** 0g; **SUGARS** 1g (est. added sugars 0g); **CHOL** 73mg; **IRON** 2mg; **SODIUM** 336mg; **CALC** 16mg

HAMBURGER STEAK
WITH ONION-MUSHROOM GRAVY

Preformed hamburger patties are easy to find but are likely made from ground chuck. This recipe uses ground sirloin, which is low in fat and high in flavor.

SERVES 4 • HANDS-ON TIME: 20 MIN. • TOTAL TIME: 30 MIN.

1   pound ground sirloin
½   teaspoon salt, divided
½   teaspoon freshly ground
     black pepper, divided
Cooking spray
1   tablespoon olive oil
1   cup vertically sliced onion

1   (8-ounce) package presliced
     cremini mushrooms
1   tablespoon all-purpose flour
1   cup unsalted beef stock
     (such as Swanson)
½   teaspoon thyme leaves

1 Shape beef into 4 (¾-inch-thick) patties; sprinkle evenly with ¼ teaspoon salt and ¼ teaspoon pepper. Coat patties with cooking spray.

2 Heat a large nonstick skillet over medium-high heat. Add patties to pan, and cook 4 minutes on each side or until browned and cooked to desired degree of doneness. Remove from pan.

3 Heat pan over medium-high heat. Add oil to pan; swirl to coat. Add onion and mushrooms to pan; sauté 7 minutes or until tender and lightly browned. Sprinkle with flour; cook, stirring constantly, 30 seconds. Add beef stock, thyme, remaining ¼ teaspoon salt, and remaining ¼ teaspoon pepper; bring to a boil, stirring constantly. Cook 1 to 2 minutes or until gravy is slightly thickened. Return patties to pan. Spoon gravy over patties. Serve immediately.

SERVING SIZE: 1 patty and 6 tablespoons gravy

CALORIES 270; **FAT** 15.2g (sat 5.1g, mono 7.6g, poly 0.9g); **PROTEIN** 25g; **CARB** 8g; **FIBER** 1g; **SUGARS** 2g (est. added sugars 0g); **CHOL** 74mg; **IRON** 3mg; **SODIUM** 406mg; **CALC** 33mg

Eat Now & Later

Crumble leftover patties, and serve with sauce over elbow noodles. Add a little chicken broth or water to loosen up the sauce if it's too thick. Throw in some roasted broccoli florets or asparagus for added crunch and extra green.

QUICK NEGIMAKI

Deli roast beef never sounded so good: Brush with sesame oil, line with cooked green onions, slather with a sweet and savory sauce, and grill.

SERVES 4 • HANDS-ON TIME: 17 MIN. • TOTAL TIME: 17 MIN.

12 thin green onions
6   thin slices deli roast beef (about 1 pound)
2   teaspoons dark sesame oil
2   tablespoons mirin (sweet rice wine)

2   tablespoons lower-sodium soy sauce
1   tablespoon sugar
Cooking spray
2   teaspoons toasted sesame seeds

1. Trim green onions to 6 inches in length. Cook onions in boiling water to cover 1 minute or just until crisp-tender but still bright green. Drain and pat dry.

2. Place beef slices on a work surface; brush with sesame oil. Place 2 green onions at one end of each slice; roll up, and secure with wooden picks.

3. Heat a grill pan over medium-high heat.

4. Combine mirin, soy sauce, and sugar in a small bowl, stirring until sugar dissolves. Coat grill pan with cooking spray. Brush beef rolls with mirin mixture; place on grill pan. Cook 3 minutes or until lightly browned, turning occasionally. Remove from pan; cut each roll in half diagonally. Drizzle with remaining mirin mixture, and sprinkle with toasted sesame seeds.

SERVING SIZE: 3 pieces

CALORIES 235; FAT 7.6g (sat 2.4g, mono 3.3g, poly 1.1g); PROTEIN 30g; CARB 9g; FIBER 1g; SUGARS 5g (est. added sugars 4g); CHOL 71mg; IRON 3mg; SODIUM 583mg; CALC 14mg

SOY-GINGER FLANK STEAK

Whip up this marinade right after breakfast so the steak can spend all day soaking up the salty, sugary goodness.

SERVES 6 • HANDS-ON TIME: 15 MIN. • TOTAL TIME: 8 HR. 25 MIN., INCLUDING MARINATE TIME

Eat Now & Later

Leftover meat and sliced green onions + ciabatta bread + stone-ground mustard = stellar steak sandwich.

⅓ cup lower-sodium soy sauce
2 tablespoons seasoned rice vinegar
1 tablespoon dark brown sugar
1 tablespoon minced peeled fresh ginger
2 teaspoons dark sesame oil
¼ teaspoon freshly ground black pepper
2 garlic cloves, minced
1 (1½-pound) flank steak, trimmed
Cooking spray
⅓ cup thinly sliced green onions
1 tablespoon toasted sesame seeds
Cilantro leaves (optional)

1 Combine first 7 ingredients in a large heavy-duty zip-top plastic bag. Add steak to bag; seal bag. Chill 8 hours, turning once.

2 Preheat grill to medium-high heat.

3 Remove steak from marinade; discard marinade. Place steak on grill rack coated with cooking spray; grill 5 minutes on each side or until desired degree of doneness. Let steak stand 10 minutes.

4 Cut steak diagonally across grain into thin slices. Sprinkle with green onions, sesame seeds, and cilantro, if desired.

SERVING SIZE: 3 ounces steak, 1 tablespoon green onions, and ½ teaspoon sesame seeds

CALORIES 183; FAT 7.6g (sat 2.4g, mono 2.5g, poly 0.5g); PROTEIN 25g; CARB 2g; FIBER 0g; SUGARS 1g (est. added sugars 1g); CHOL 70mg; IRON 2mg; SODIUM 208mg; CALC 31mg

HERB-CRUSTED PORK TENDERLOIN WITH ONIONS

Break out the gin for a bright, buttery pan sauce that turns a platter of pork into a decadent dinner alongside roasted potatoes and asparagus spears.

SERVES 4 • HANDS-ON TIME: 25 MIN. • TOTAL TIME: 30 MIN.

¼ cup chopped fresh parsley
2 tablespoons refrigerated reduced-fat pesto
1 tablespoon chopped fresh rosemary
1 (1-pound) pork tenderloin, trimmed
Cooking spray

1 cup thin vertical slices sweet onion
¼ cup fat-free, lower-sodium chicken broth
3 tablespoons gin
1 tablespoon fresh lemon juice
2 teaspoons butter

1 Preheat oven to 400°F.

2 Combine first 3 ingredients in a small bowl; rub surface of tenderloin with herb mixture. Heat a large nonstick skillet over medium-high heat. Coat tenderloin with cooking spray; add to pan. Cook 1 minute on all sides or until browned.

3 Remove pan from heat; transfer tenderloin to a rimmed baking sheet lined with foil and coated with cooking spray. Bake, uncovered, at 400°F for 10 minutes or until a thermometer registers 145°F (slightly pink). Place tenderloin on a platter; let stand 10 minutes.

4 Return skillet to heat; add onion to pan. Sauté over medium-high heat 5 minutes or until tender and beginning to brown. Add chicken broth and gin. Bring to a boil, scraping pan to loosen browned bits. Cook 1 minute or until liquid is reduced and coats onion. Remove from heat; add lemon juice and butter, stirring until butter melts. Cut tenderloin into slices; serve with onion sauce.

SERVING SIZE: 3 ounces pork and ¾ cup onion sauce

CALORIES 214; FAT 7.2g (sat 2.6g, mono 3.1g, poly 0.6g); PROTEIN 25g; CARB 5g; FIBER 1g; SUGARS 2g (est. added sugars 0g); CHOL 81mg; IRON 2mg; SODIUM 182mg; CALC 45mg

Eat Now & Later

Leftover pork tenderloin and onion practically beg to be turned into tacos. Warm small tortillas, add pork and onion, and top with cheese and salsa for a quick and easy lunch tomorrow.

PORK BANH MI TARTINE

This open-faced version of a Vietnamese favorite is a smart way to enjoy all the exciting flavors and textures of the classic sandwich while skipping some of the calories.

SERVES 4 • HANDS-ON TIME: 25 MIN. • TOTAL TIME: 25 MIN.

Savvy Shortcuts

To save prep time, buy precut vegetables, or use a mandoline or the slicing attachment of your food processor to julienne and slice them A.S.A.P.

1   cup rice vinegar
¼   cup sugar
2   teaspoons salt
1   cup matchstick-cut carrots
1   cup julienne-cut daikon radish
½   cup julienne-cut red onion
2   tablespoons canola mayonnaise
2   tablespoons Sriracha (hot chile sauce, such as Huy Fong)
2   (3⅛-ounce) French bread rolls, halved lengthwise

Cooking spray
12   ounces thinly sliced deli roasted pork loin
1   cup coarsely chopped cilantro leaves
1   cup coarsely chopped basil leaves
1   cup thin English cucumber slices
1   (1-ounce) jalapeño pepper, thinly sliced

1 Preheat oven to 375°F.

2 Combine vinegar, sugar, and salt in a medium microwave-safe bowl. Microwave, uncovered, at HIGH 10 to 15 seconds or until sugar and salt dissolve, stirring after 10 seconds.

3 Add carrots, radish, and onion. Let stand 12 minutes, stirring occasionally. Drain, discarding marinade.

4 Combine mayonnaise and Sriracha in a small bowl, stirring to blend.

5 Coat cut sides of roll halves with cooking spray, and place on a baking sheet. Bake at 375°F for 5 minutes or until toasted.

6 Remove baking sheet from oven. Spread 1 tablespoon mayonnaise mixture on cut side of each roll half. Layer 3 ounces pork on top of mayonnaise mixture on each roll half. Return to oven; bake 5 additional minutes or until pork is thoroughly heated.

7 Combine cilantro and basil in a medium bowl. Place ¼ cup cucumber slices on top of pork, overlapping slightly. Top sandwiches evenly with jalapeño slices; top each with ½ cup cilantro mixture and ½ cup marinated vegetables. Serve immediately.

SERVING SIZE: 1 tartine

CALORIES 356; FAT 12.2g (sat 3.2g, mono 5.3g, poly 2.2g); PROTEIN 30g; CARB 29g; FIBER 2g; SUGARS 6g (est. added sugars 3g); CHOL 72mg; IRON 3mg; SODIUM 577mg; CALC 107mg

ROASTED PORK TENDERLOIN
WITH SPICY MANGO SAUCE

This stovetop-to-oven method of cooking pork yields a moist and tender piece of meat you can cut with your fork.

SERVES 6 • HANDS-ON TIME: 10 MIN. • TOTAL TIME: 3 HR. 35 MIN., INCLUDING MARINATE TIME

¼ cup rice vinegar, divided
3 tablespoons lower-sodium soy sauce
2 tablespoons brown sugar
2 teaspoons grated peeled fresh ginger
2 teaspoons chile paste with garlic (such as sambal oelek)
2 large garlic cloves, minced

1 (1½-pound) pork tenderloin, trimmed
¼ teaspoon salt
¼ teaspoon freshly ground black pepper
2 teaspoons canola oil
3 tablespoons hot mango chutney (such as Major Grey's)
1 tablespoon water

1 Combine 3 tablespoons rice vinegar and next 5 ingredients (through garlic) in a large heavy-duty zip-top plastic bag. Add pork tenderloin; seal bag, and marinate in refrigerator 3 hours, turning bag occasionally. Remove pork from bag; discard marinade. Sprinkle pork with salt and pepper.

2 Preheat oven to 425°F.

3 Heat an ovenproof skillet over medium-high heat. Add oil to pan; swirl to coat. Add pork; cook 4 minutes, turning to brown on all sides. Transfer skillet to oven. Bake at 425°F for 15 minutes or until a thermometer registers 145°F (slightly pink). Remove from oven. Cover and let stand 10 minutes.

4 While pork bakes, place chutney, 1 tablespoon water, and remaining 1 tablespoon rice vinegar in blender; process 30 seconds or until smooth. Stir in any accumulated pan juices.

5 Cut pork crosswise into ¼-inch-thick slices. Serve with sauce.

SERVING SIZE: 3 ounces pork and 2½ teaspoons sauce

CALORIES 171; **FAT** 4g (sat 0.9g, mono 1.9g, poly 0.9g); **PROTEIN** 24g; **CARB** 8g; **FIBER** 0g; **SUGARS** 8g (est. added sugars 4g); **CHOL** 74mg; **IRON** 1mg; **SODIUM** 351mg; **CALC** 8mg

Eat Now & Later

Beans and rice from the supermarket hot bar make a fantastic base for leftover pork and mango chutney. If you have fresh cilantro on hand, toss a few leaves on top.

JERK PORK MEDALLIONS
WITH MANGO SALSA

Something as simple as Caribbean seasoning and fruity salsa transforms pork tenderloin from plain to provocative in a matter of minutes. Black beans and rice make it a meal.

SERVES 4 • HANDS-ON TIME: 13 MIN. • TOTAL TIME: 13 MIN.

➡️ **Savvy Shortcuts**

Savvy Shortcuts

Adding chopped fresh mango into prepared salsa saves many steps, but you can skip them altogether and find freshly made mango salsa in the produce or deli section of your supermarket.

1   (1-pound) pork tenderloin, cut into 12 slices
½   teaspoon salt
1   tablespoon salt-free jerk seasoning (such as Penzey's)
2   tablespoons olive oil, divided

1   cup fresh salsa
1   small peeled ripe mango, diced (about 1 cup)
1   tablespoon chopped fresh cilantro
½   teaspoon grated lime rind
4   lime wedges

1 Flatten pork pieces to ½-inch thickness using fingertips. Sprinkle both sides of pork with salt and jerk seasoning. Heat a large nonstick skillet over medium-high heat. Add 1 tablespoon oil to pan; swirl to coat. Add half of pork to pan; cook 2 minutes on each side or until browned. Transfer pork to a serving platter. Repeat procedure with remaining oil and pork.

2 Combine salsa and remaining ingredients except lime wedges in a small bowl. Serve with pork and lime wedges.

SERVING SIZE: 3 pork slices, about ½ cup salsa, and 1 lime wedge
CALORIES 233; FAT 9.4g (sat 1.8g, mono 5.9g, poly 1.2g); PROTEIN 24g; CARB 11g; FIBER 1g; SUGARS 11g (est. added sugars 0g); CHOL 74mg; IRON 1mg; SODIUM 572mg; CALC 52mg

PORK TENDERLOIN AND FIGS
WITH SORGHUM-BALSAMIC GLAZE

Whip up this simple sweet-and-sour glaze while the seared pork rests. Serve with Bacon and Cheddar Mashed Potatoes (page 162) and Roasted Baby Spring Vegetables (page 149) for a weeknight meal that feels fancy.

SERVES 4 • HANDS-ON TIME: 17 MIN. • TOTAL TIME: 32 MIN.

1 cup hot water
½ cup dried Mission figlets, quartered
1 (1-pound) pork tenderloin, trimmed
¼ teaspoon kosher salt
½ teaspoon freshly ground
   black pepper
2 teaspoons olive oil

¼ cup chopped shallots
¼ cup fat-free, lower-sodium
   chicken broth
¼ cup sorghum
2 tablespoons balsamic vinegar
2 teaspoons butter
½ teaspoon chopped fresh thyme

1 Preheat oven to 400°F.

2 Combine 1 cup hot water and figlet pieces in a small bowl. Let stand 10 minutes or until softened. Drain, reserving ¼ cup liquid.

3 Pat pork dry; sprinkle salt and pepper over surface of pork. Heat a large nonstick skillet over medium-high heat. Add oil to pan; swirl to coat. Add pork to pan; cook 6 minutes, turning to brown all sides. Remove pan from heat; transfer pork to a foil-lined baking sheet. Bake at 400°F for 12 minutes or until a thermometer registers 140°F. Cover and let stand 10 minutes or until thermometer registers 145°F (slightly pink).

4 While pork cooks, add shallots to skillet; return pan to medium heat. Sauté 1 to 2 minutes or until shallots are slightly tender. Add chicken broth, sorghum, vinegar, and reserved figlet liquid; cook 1 minute, scraping pan to loosen browned bits. Bring to a boil; reduce heat, and simmer, uncovered, 1 minute or until reduced to ½ cup. Add drained figlet pieces, butter, and thyme, stirring until butter melts. Remove pan from heat.

5 Cut pork into slices. Serve with sauce.

SERVING SIZE: about 3 ounces pork and 3 tablespoons sauce

CALORIES 285; FAT 6.7g (sat 2.3g, mono 3g, poly 0.7g); PROTEIN 25g; CARB 30g; FIBER 3g; SUGARS 26g (est. added sugars 15g); CHOL 79mg; IRON 3mg; SODIUM 236mg; CALC 71mg

LEMONGRASS PORK SKEWERS

Found in most supermarkets, lemongrass adds minty citrus notes to this Vietnamese-style pork dish. Serve it with rice noodles and Roasted Baby Spring Vegetables (page 149) for a complete meal.

SERVES 4 • HANDS-ON TIME: 15 MIN. • TOTAL TIME: 1 HR. 15 MIN., INCLUDING MARINATE TIME

Fast Freeze

Lemongrass loves the freezer: Cut the edible part into small sections, and store in a freezer bag or airtight container up to four to six months.

¼ cup coarsely chopped peeled fresh lemongrass (1 stalk)
2 tablespoons light brown sugar
2 tablespoons fish sauce
1 tablespoon lower-sodium soy sauce
1 tablespoon peanut oil
3 large garlic cloves
¼ teaspoon freshly ground black pepper
1 small shallot, peeled and quartered
1 (1-pound) pork tenderloin, trimmed and cut into 16 (1½-inch) pieces
Cooking spray
Chopped fresh cilantro (optional)
4 lime wedges

1 Place first 8 ingredients in a blender or food processor; process until smooth. Place mixture in a large heavy-duty zip-top plastic bag; add pork. Seal bag, and marinate in refrigerator 1 hour, turning occasionally.

2 Preheat grill to medium-high heat.

3 Remove pork from bag; discard marinade. Thread pork onto 4 (8-inch) metal skewers. Place skewers on grill rack coated with cooking spray; grill 2 to 3 minutes on each side or until lightly charred and done. Garnish with cilantro, if desired, and serve with lime wedges.

SERVING SIZE: 1 skewer and 1 lime wedge

CALORIES 175; FAT 4.9g (sat 1.2g, mono 2.1g, poly 1.2g); PROTEIN 25g; CARB 7g; FIBER 0g; SUGARS 5g (est. added sugars 4g); CHOL 74mg; IRON 2mg; SODIUM 594mg; CALC 18mg

LAMB SLIDERS
WITH FETA AND MINTED YOGURT SAUCE

Bored with the same old burger? Think small—serve lamb sliders on grilled pita bread instead of a bun. Just don't let the size of these fool you—they're big on flavor and sure to fill you up.

SERVES 4 • HANDS-ON TIME: 21 MIN. • TOTAL TIME: 31 MIN.

1   pound lean ground lamb
2   ounces crumbled feta cheese (about ½ cup)
1   tablespoon grated fresh onion
2   teaspoons chopped fresh oregano
⅓   cup 2% reduced-fat Greek yogurt (such as Fage)
1½ teaspoons chopped fresh mint
½   teaspoon grated lemon rind
2   teaspoons fresh lemon juice
1   garlic clove, minced
¼   teaspoon salt
¼   teaspoon freshly ground black pepper
Cooking spray
4   (1-ounce) mini whole-wheat pitas, halved lengthwise
1   bunch curly leaf lettuce
1⅓ cups premade cucumber-tomato salad with red onion (about 8 ounces; such as Whole Foods olive bar)

1 Preheat grill to medium-high heat.

2 Combine first 4 ingredients in a medium bowl. Shape mixture into 4 (½-inch-thick) patties. Place patties on a waxed paper-lined pan; cover and chill 10 minutes.

3 Combine yogurt and next 4 ingredients (through garlic) in a small bowl.

4 Sprinkle lamb patties evenly with salt and pepper. Place lamb patties on grill rack coated with cooking spray. Grill 4 to 5 minutes on each side or until a thermometer registers 160°F.

5 Add pita halves to grill rack; grill 30 seconds on each side. Top bottom half of each pita with lettuce, 1 lamb patty, ⅓ cup cucumber-tomato salad, and 1½ tablespoons yogurt sauce. Cover with pita tops.

SERVING SIZE: 1 lamb slider

CALORIES 355; FAT 15.2g (sat 6.2g, mono 3.5g, poly 1g); PROTEIN 32g; CARB 21g; FIBER 3g; SUGARS 5g (est. added sugars 1g); CHOL 98mg; IRON 2mg; SODIUM 599mg; CALC 123mg

GRILLED BONELESS LEG OF LAMB

When winter finally makes an exit, fire up the grill for a true taste of spring. This succulent lamb is finished off with a drizzle of olive oil, a sprinkling of flaky sea salt, chopped fresh mint, and fresh lemon.

SERVES 6 • HANDS-ON TIME: 23 MIN. • TOTAL TIME: 1 HR. 33 MIN., INCLUDING MARINATE TIME

Savvy Shortcuts

To ensure quick and even grilling, have your supermarket butcher butterfly the boneless leg of lamb to uniform thickness.

1¾ pounds boneless leg of lamb, trimmed
2½ tablespoons fresh lemon juice
1 tablespoon chopped fresh oregano
2 teaspoons chopped fresh rosemary
6 garlic cloves, crushed
¼ cup olive oil, divided
½ teaspoon kosher salt
¼ teaspoon freshly ground black pepper
Cooking spray
¼ teaspoon sea salt flakes (such as Maldon)
¼ cup chopped fresh mint
6 lemon wedges

1 Cut horizontally through center of lamb, cutting to, but not through, other side using a sharp knife; open flat as you would a book. Place lamb between 2 sheets of plastic wrap; pound to an even thickness using a meat mallet or small heavy skillet.

2 Combine lemon juice, oregano, rosemary, garlic, and 3 tablespoons olive oil in a large heavy-duty zip-top plastic bag. Add lamb; seal bag, and marinate at room temperature 1 hour, turning bag occasionally. Remove lamb from bag, discarding marinade.

3 Preheat grill to medium-high heat.

4 Sprinkle lamb with kosher salt and pepper. Place lamb on grill rack coated with cooking spray; grill 5 minutes on each side, or until a thermometer registers 145°F (medium-rare). Cover and let stand 10 minutes.

5 Cut lamb across grain into thin slices; arrange on a serving platter. Drizzle lamb with remaining 1 tablespoon olive oil; sprinkle with sea salt and mint. Serve with lemon wedges.

SERVING SIZE: 3½ ounces lamb and 1 lemon wedge

CALORIES 225; FAT 11.7g (sat 2.9g, mono 6.5g, poly 1.2g); PROTEIN 27g; CARB 2g; FIBER 0g; SUGARS 0g (est. added sugars 0g); CHOL 85mg; IRON 3mg; SODIUM 340mg; CALC 16mg

CREOLE SHRIMP
WITH ANDOUILLE

Channel the best of New Orleans cuisine in this traditional Creole dish, filled with spicy chicken and turkey andouille sausage.

SERVES 6 • HANDS-ON TIME: 25 MIN. • TOTAL TIME: 25 MIN.

1   (5.2-ounce) bag boil-in-bag long-grain rice
½   (12-ounce) package chicken and turkey andouille sausage, cut into ¼-inch-thick slices
2   (8-ounce) packages refrigerated prechopped onion, bell pepper, and celery
Cooking spray
1⅓ cups fat-free, lower-sodium chicken broth
2   teaspoons salt-free Creole seasoning

¼   teaspoon ground red pepper
¼   teaspoon salt
3   large garlic cloves, minced
1   (14½-ounce) can unsalted diced tomatoes, undrained
2   tablespoons all-purpose flour
¼   cup water
1   pound medium shrimp, peeled and deveined
⅓   cup sliced green onions
¼   cup chopped fresh parsley

1 Cook rice according to package directions.

2 While rice cooks, heat a large nonstick skillet over medium-high heat. Add sausage; cook 3 minutes or until lightly browned, stirring frequently. Remove sausage from pan.

3 Add celery mixture to pan; coat with cooking spray, and sauté 5 minutes. Add chicken broth and next 5 ingredients (through tomatoes). Bring to a boil; reduce heat, and simmer, uncovered, 5 minutes.

4 Combine flour and ¼ cup water in a small bowl, stirring with a whisk; add to broth mixture. Bring to a boil; cook, stirring constantly, 1 minute or until thick. Add shrimp; cook 4 minutes or until shrimp are done. Stir in sausage, green onions, and parsley; cook 1 minute or until thoroughly heated.

SERVING SIZE: 1 cup shrimp mixture and ½ cup rice

CALORIES 248; FAT 3.9g (sat 0.9g, mono 0.9g, poly 0.7g); PROTEIN 20g; CARB 33g; FIBER 4g; SUGARS 5g (est. added sugars 0g); CHOL 117mg; IRON 4mg; SODIUM 619mg; CALC 110mg

SEARED SALMON
WITH HOISIN GLAZE

The best thing about salmon—besides its mega-dose of omega-3s—
is the way the crispy top layer gives way to tender flakes. Serve on
a bed of Spicy Sesame-Garlic Spinach (page 154) or with steamed,
chilled broccoli on the side.

SERVES 4 • HANDS-ON TIME: 13 MIN. • TOTAL TIME: 13 MIN.

¼ cup apple juice
2 tablespoons hoisin sauce
1 tablespoon fresh lime juice
1 teaspoon lower-sodium soy sauce
1 teaspoon chili garlic sauce
   (such as Lee Kum Kee)

1 teaspoon ginger paste
1 tablespoon canola oil
4 (6-ounce) salmon fillets
   (about 1 inch thick)
½ cup torn cilantro leaves
2 tablespoons toasted sesame seeds

1 Preheat oven to 350°F.

2 Place first 6 ingredients in a small saucepan. Bring to a simmer over medium-high heat. Cook, uncovered, 2 minutes or until reduced to ¼ cup. Remove from heat.

3 Heat a large nonstick skillet over medium-high heat. Add oil to pan; swirl to coat. Add fillets, skin side up, to pan. Cook 4 minutes or until lightly browned. Turn fillets over; reduce heat to medium, and cook 2 minutes.

4 Transfer fillets to a foil-lined baking sheet. Spoon half of hoisin glaze over fillets. Bake at 350°F for 5 minutes or until fillets are desired degree of doneness and glaze thickens.

5 Drizzle remaining half of glaze over salmon; sprinkle evenly with cilantro and sesame seeds.

SERVING SIZE: 1 fillet, 2 tablespoons cilantro, and 1½ teaspoons sesame seeds

CALORIES 310; FAT 13.7g (sat 1.7g, mono 4.6g, poly 2.5g); PROTEIN 36g; CARB 7g; FIBER 1g; SUGARS 4g
(est. added sugars 2g); CHOL 78mg; IRON 1mg; SODIUM 392mg; CALC 28mg

SEARED SCALLOPS
WITH ASPARAGUS AND PEAS IN LEMON SAUCE

A little butter and a hot pan are all you need to sear the sweet meat of the scallop to perfection. Add in a bit of white wine, shallots, lemon juice, and tender green veggies, and you take them to another level entirely.

SERVES 4 • HANDS-ON TIME: 17 MIN. • TOTAL TIME: 17 MIN.

½ pound large asparagus spears
1 tablespoon olive oil
2 tablespoons butter, divided
12 large sea scallops (about 1½ pounds)
¼ teaspoon freshly ground black pepper
⅛ teaspoon salt

¼ cup chopped shallots
¼ cup white wine
1 teaspoon grated lemon rind
2 tablespoons fresh lemon juice
1 cup frozen petite green peas, thawed

1 Snap off tough ends of asparagus. Trim tips from asparagus spears (about ¾ inch from tip end); cut spears diagonally into ¼-inch-thick slices.

2 Heat olive oil and 1 tablespoon butter in a large nonstick skillet over medium-high heat until butter melts. Pat scallops dry; sprinkle with pepper and salt. Add scallops to pan; cook 3 minutes on each side or until done. Remove scallops from pan; keep warm.

3 Add shallots to pan; sauté 1 minute. Add asparagus, wine, lemon rind, lemon juice, and remaining 1 tablespoon butter; sauté 1 minute. Add peas; cook 1 minute or until asparagus is crisp-tender.

4 Spoon vegetable mixture into 4 bowls; top evenly with scallops.

SERVING SIZE: ½ cup vegetable mixture and 3 scallops

CALORIES 244; **FAT** 10g (sat 4.4g, mono 4g, poly 0.8g); **PROTEIN** 23g; **CARB** 13g; **FIBER** 3g; **SUGARS** 3g (est. added sugars 0g); **CHOL** 56mg; **IRON** 2mg; **SODIUM** 446mg; **CALC** 32mg

Seasonal Switch-Up

Thinly sliced napa cabbage or leeks keep the green going strong when spring asparagus is out of season.

SHRIMP "CEVICHE"

Ceviche is traditionally made of raw fish "cooked" in citrus juices. This version speeds up the process with precooked shrimp while eliciting the same lively flavors. Serve with Bibb lettuce leaves, if you like.

SERVES 4 • HANDS-ON TIME: 10 MIN. • TOTAL TIME: 20 MIN.

Savvy Shortcuts

Check your fish counter for cooked shrimp, or ask your fishmonger to steam fresh, raw shrimp while you shop.

1 pound cooked peeled and deveined medium shrimp
2 cups refrigerated chunky hot salsa (such as La Mexicana)
1¼ cups diced English cucumber
2 tablespoons chopped fresh cilantro
1 tablespoon fresh lime juice
1 tablespoon fresh lemon juice
⅛ teaspoon salt
¼ teaspoon freshly ground black pepper
1 ripe peeled avocado, diced
4 lime wedges

1 Pat shrimp dry, and cut into ½-inch pieces.

2 Drain salsa, discarding liquid. Combine salsa, cucumber, and remaining ingredients except lime wedges in a large bowl. Add shrimp; toss gently. Serve with lime wedges.

NOTE: We do not recommend using frozen cooked shrimp for this recipe.

SERVING SIZE: 1 cup shrimp mixture and 1 lime wedge

CALORIES 209; FAT 8.6g (sat 1.2g, mono 5g, poly 1.1g); PROTEIN 17g; CARB 12g; FIBER 4g; SUGARS 5g (est. added sugars 0g); CHOL 143mg; IRON 1mg; SODIUM 545mg; CALC 76mg

SEARED SNAPPER
WITH OLIVE-BAR PAN SAUCE

Grab a few marinated cipollini onions, Peppadew peppers, and gorgeous green Castelvetrano olives at your supermarket olive bar, and put them to work as the salty stars of this seared fish dish.

SERVES 4 • HANDS-ON TIME: 21 MIN. • TOTAL TIME: 21 MIN.

2 tablespoons canola oil
4 (6-ounce) red snapper fillets (¾ inch thick)
¼ teaspoon salt
½ teaspoon freshly ground black pepper
2 tablespoons chopped shallots
2 tablespoons chopped marinated cipollini onions (about 2 small onions; such as Whole Foods olive bar)
2 tablespoons chopped Peppadew peppers (about 3 peppers; such as Whole Foods olive bar)
8 pitted Castelvetrano olives, chopped (such as Whole Foods olive bar)
1 tablespoon fresh lemon juice
2 tablespoons chopped fresh parsley
2 teaspoons butter

1 Preheat oven to 200°F.

2 Heat a large nonstick skillet over medium-high heat. Add oil to pan; swirl to coat. Pat fish dry with paper towels. Add fish, skin side down, to pan; sprinkle with salt and pepper. Cook 4 minutes or until skin is crisp, pressing fish down with a spatula to prevent curling. Turn fish over; reduce heat to medium. Cook 3 minutes or until fish flakes easily when tested with a fork. Remove from pan; keep warm.

3 Add shallots to pan; sauté 1 minute. Add onions, peppers, and olives; sauté 1 minute. Add lemon juice, parsley, and butter, stirring until butter melts. Place 1 fish fillet on each of 4 plates. Spoon olive mixture evenly over fish.

SERVING SIZE: 1 fillet and 2 tablespoons olive mixture

CALORIES 287; FAT 13.3g (sat 2.5g, mono 5.4g, poly 2.8g); PROTEIN 35g; CARB 5g; FIBER 1g; SUGARS 3g (est. added sugars 0g); CHOL 68mg; IRON 1mg; SODIUM 392mg; CALC 61mg

GRILLED SHRIMP KEBABS
WITH CHARRED TOMATO VINAIGRETTE AND FETA

Don't let a drop of this incredible vinaigrette go to waste: Use any leftovers to dress a fresh green salad.

SERVES 4 • HANDS-ON TIME: 25 MIN. • TOTAL TIME: 25 MIN.

32 large shrimp (1¾ pounds), peeled and deveined

Cooking spray

⅜ teaspoon kosher salt, divided

1 teaspoon freshly ground black pepper, divided

4 plum tomatoes, halved lengthwise

1 ounce crumbled feta cheese (about ¼ cup)

¼ cup olive oil

2 tablespoons chopped shallots

1½ tablespoons sherry vinegar

1 tablespoon chopped fresh thyme

➊ Preheat grill to medium-high heat.

➋ Thread 8 shrimp onto each of 4 (12-inch) skewers. Coat skewers with cooking spray; sprinkle evenly with ⅛ teaspoon salt and ½ teaspoon pepper. Coat tomato halves with cooking spray.

➌ Place tomato halves on grill rack; grill 4 minutes. Turn tomatoes over; add skewers to grill rack. Grill skewers 3 minutes on each side or until shrimp are done and tomatoes are lightly charred. Transfer skewers to a serving platter; sprinkle with cheese.

➍ Place tomatoes, olive oil, shallots, vinegar, thyme, remaining ¼ teaspoon salt, and remaining ½ teaspoon pepper in a blender; process until smooth. Serve kebabs with tomato vinaigrette.

SERVING SIZE: 1 kebab, ¼ cup vinaigrette, and 1 tablespoon cheese

CALORIES 313; FAT 18.3g (sat 3.6g, mono 10.8g, poly 2g); PROTEIN 29g; CARB 7g; FIBER 2g; SUGARS 4g (est. added sugars 0g); CHOL 258mg; IRON 1mg; SODIUM 565mg; CALC 170mg

SPICY SHAKSHUKA
OVER GARLIC GREENS

Arabic for "mixture," shakshuka is the ultimate breakfast-for-dinner dish. Serve with toasted flatbread or naan to sop up every bit of the rich, spicy sauce.

SERVES 6 • HANDS-ON TIME: 23 MIN. • TOTAL TIME: 23 MIN.

1 cup refrigerated prechopped tricolor bell peppers
1 cup refrigerated prechopped onion
Cooking spray
¼ cup halved pitted kalamata olives
¼ teaspoon smoked paprika
1 (24-ounce) jar fra diavolo sauce or other spicy pasta sauce (such as Rao's Arrabbiata)

6 large eggs
½ teaspoon freshly ground black pepper
⅛ teaspoon kosher salt
1 ounce crumbled feta cheese (about ¼ cup)
2 teaspoons olive oil
2 garlic cloves, chopped
2 (5-ounce) containers prewashed baby kale and spinach blend

1 Preheat oven to 400°F.

2 Heat a large ovenproof nonstick skillet over medium-high heat. Add bell peppers and onion; coat vegetables with cooking spray. Cook, stirring often, 6 minutes or until tender and lightly browned. Stir in olives, smoked paprika, and pasta sauce; bring to a simmer. Remove pan from heat.

3 Break eggs into sauce, spacing evenly apart. Sprinkle eggs with pepper and salt. Sprinkle with cheese. (Do not stir.) Place skillet on rack in upper third of oven. Bake at 400°F for 12 minutes or until whites are set.

4 While eggs cook, heat a large Dutch oven over medium-high heat. Add oil to pan; swirl to coat. Add garlic; sauté 30 seconds. Add greens, stirring until wilted.

5 Place greens on each of 6 plates. Top each serving with an egg and sauce.

SERVING SIZE: ⅓ cup greens, 1 egg, and ⅔ cup sauce

CALORIES 237; FAT 15.6g (sat 3.9g, mono 6.1g, poly 3.6g); PROTEIN 10g; CARB 13g; FIBER 3g; SUGARS 6g (est. added sugars 0g); CHOL 192mg; IRON 5mg; SODIUM 653mg; CALC 137mg

TOMATOES, MUSHROOMS, AND ZUCCHINI
OVER CREAMY PESTO POLENTA

Polenta is the new pasta. It cooks up in minutes and creates a creamy base for this vegetarian dinner that's so hearty you won't miss the meat.

SERVES 4 • HANDS-ON TIME: 8 MIN. • TOTAL TIME: 29 MIN.

¼ cup boiling water
2 tablespoons chopped smoked sun-dried tomatoes, packed without oil
4 cups water
1 cup instant polenta
2 tablespoons refrigerated reduced-fat pesto
2 ounces shaved fresh Parmesan cheese (about ½ cup), divided
1 tablespoon canola oil

1 (8-ounce) package presliced cremini mushrooms
¼ teaspoon salt
¼ teaspoon freshly ground black pepper
1 medium zucchini, cut into ¼-inch-thick half-moon-shaped slices (1¾ cups)
2 garlic cloves
1 cup halved grape tomatoes (about 6 ounces)
2 teaspoons butter

1 Combine ¼ cup boiling water and sun-dried tomatoes in a small bowl. Let stand about 10 minutes or until soft.

2 Bring 4 cups water to a boil in a medium saucepan. Gradually add polenta, stirring with a whisk. Cook, stirring constantly with a whisk, 2 to 3 minutes or until thick. Remove from heat; stir in pesto and ¼ cup cheese. Cover and keep warm.

3 Heat a large nonstick skillet over high heat. Add canola oil to pan; swirl to coat. Add mushrooms, salt, and pepper; sauté 8 minutes or until mushrooms are lightly browned. Add zucchini and garlic; sauté 4 minutes or until zucchini is lightly browned. Add grape tomatoes; sauté 4 minutes. Stir in sun-dried tomatoes and soaking liquid; cook 1 minute or until liquid almost evaporates. Add butter, stirring until melted. Remove from heat.

4 Spoon polenta into each of 4 bowls; top evenly with vegetable mixture, and sprinkle evenly with remaining ¼ cup cheese.

SERVING SIZE: 1 cup polenta, ¾ cup vegetable mixture, and 1 tablespoon cheese
CALORIES 331; FAT 11.9g (sat 4.5g, mono 4g, poly 1.2g); PROTEIN 13g; CARB 44g; FIBER 6g; SUGARS 6g (est. added sugars 0g); CHOL 17mg; IRON 5mg; SODIUM 484mg; CALC 225mg

SPICY-HUMMUS GRILLED VEGGIE WRAP

The best of the summer harvest comes together in this meatless sandwich laced with Sriracha-carrot hummus. Make ahead and refrigerate for a filling dinner on the go.

SERVES 4 • HANDS-ON TIME: 15 MIN. • TOTAL TIME: 15 MIN.

1   medium zucchini, thinly sliced lengthwise

1   small yellow squash, thinly sliced lengthwise

1   Japanese eggplant, thinly sliced lengthwise

1   red bell pepper, quartered and seeded

Cooking spray

¼   teaspoon salt

¼   teaspoon freshly ground black pepper

4   (1.7-ounce) light flatbreads (such as Flatout)

¾   cup Sriracha-carrot hummus (such as Eat Well Embrace Life)

4   roasted tomato halves, coarsely chopped (such as Whole Foods)

2   ounces crumbled feta cheese (about ½ cup)

1 Preheat grill to medium-high heat.

2 Lightly coat first 4 ingredients with cooking spray. Sprinkle evenly with salt and black pepper. Place on grill rack coated with cooking spray; grill, in 2 batches, 3 minutes on each side or until tender.

3 Spread 1 side of each flatbread with 3 tablespoons hummus. Divide grilled vegetables and roasted tomatoes evenly over hummus. Sprinkle each flatbread with 2 tablespoons crumbled feta. Roll up flatbreads, jelly-roll fashion, starting with short sides. Cut diagonally into slices, if desired.

SERVING SIZE: 1 wrap

CALORIES 290; FAT 14.2g (sat 3g, mono 3.7g, poly 2.3g); PROTEIN 17g; CARB 34g; FIBER 14g; SUGARS 10g (est. added sugars 1g); CHOL 17mg; IRON 3mg; SODIUM 753mg; CALC 158mg

CHAPTER 3

SUPERFAST SIDES

Choosing sides can be tricky. We want them to be delicious but also complement the entrée. To come together quickly but taste like they developed over time. To be healthy but deliciously decadent. And to come with a short list of ingredients that doesn't require a supermarket treasure hunt.

Recipes that fit the above requirements do exist—and they're in this chapter. From Browned-Butter Gnocchi to Roasted Baby Artichokes with Lemon Aioli, our Superfast Sides give you the best of both worlds. Flip through, find a few, and cook yourself right out of that recipe rut.

ROASTED BRUSSELS SPROUTS WITH HAM AND GARLIC

Break out of the Brussels-and-bacon mold with country ham, which imparts salty pork flavor without the competing crunch.

SERVES 12 • HANDS-ON TIME: 7 MIN. • TOTAL TIME: 37 MIN.

➤ **Savvy Shortcuts**

Skip Steps 1 and 2, and purchase premade breadcrumbs at the store. If your supermarket has a bakery section, look for fresh breadcrumbs sold by the bag.

1 (1-ounce) slice white bread
3 pounds Brussels sprouts, trimmed and halved
¼ cup finely chopped country ham (about 1 ounce)
2 tablespoons fresh lemon juice
1 teaspoon olive oil
½ teaspoon salt
3 garlic cloves, thinly sliced
Cooking spray
2 tablespoons grated fresh Parmesan cheese

❶ Preheat oven to 425°F.

❷ Place bread in a food processor; pulse 2 times or until crumbly. Sprinkle crumbs on a baking sheet; bake at 425°F for 5 minutes or until golden. Reduce oven temperature to 375°F. Set aside 3 tablespoons toasted breadcrumbs, reserving remaining breadcrumbs for another use.

❸ Combine Brussels sprouts and next 5 ingredients (through garlic) in a 3-quart baking dish coated with cooking spray, tossing to coat. Bake at 375°F for 30 minutes or until Brussels sprouts are tender and lightly browned on edges, stirring twice.

❹ Combine 3 tablespoons reserved breadcrumbs and Parmesan cheese; sprinkle over Brussels sprouts. Serve immediately.

SERVING SIZE: ¾ cup

CALORIES 68; FAT 1.2g; (sat 0.4g, mono 0.5g, poly 0.2g); PROTEIN 5g; CARB 12g; FIBER 4g; SUGARS 3g (est. added sugars 0g); CHOL 2mg; IRON 1mg; SODIUM 215mg; CALC 65mg

ROASTED BABY SPRING VEGETABLES

White balsamic vinegar tames the sweetness of roasted veggies without dulling their bright, beautiful colors.

SERVES 7 • HANDS-ON TIME: 10 MIN. • TOTAL TIME: 35 MIN.

3   tablespoons white balsamic vinegar
1   tablespoon chopped shallots
1   pound baby carrots with tops
1   tablespoon olive oil
½   teaspoon salt
¼   teaspoon freshly ground black pepper
12 fingerling potatoes, halved lengthwise (about 1¼ pounds)
1   (6-ounce) bag radishes, halved (about 1¾ cups)
2   cups (2-inch) slices asparagus (about 1 pound)
1   tablespoon chopped fresh flat-leaf parsley
1   tablespoon chopped fresh chives

1 Preheat oven to 500°F.

2 Combine vinegar and shallots in a small bowl; set aside.

3 Trim green tops from carrots; discard tops. Combine carrots and next 5 ingredients (through radishes) in the bottom of a roasting pan, tossing gently to combine. Bake at 500°F for 20 minutes or until vegetables begin to brown, stirring occasionally. Remove pan from the oven; add shallot mixture and asparagus, tossing to combine. Return pan to oven; bake 5 minutes. Stir in parsley and chives.

SERVING SIZE: 1 cup

CALORIES 126; Fat 2.2g (sat 0.3g, mono 1.4g, poly 0.3g); **PROTEIN** 4g; **CARB** 25g; **FIBER** 5g; **SUGARS** 7g (est. added sugars 0g); **CHOL** 0mg; **IRON** 3mg; **SODIUM** 239mg; **CALCIUM** 54mg

Eat Now & Later

Hash it out: Chop up the leftovers, warm them through, and put a **poached egg** on top for a hearty, healthy meal any time of the day.

FRIED BROWN RICE
WITH RED PEPPER AND ALMONDS

Take your wok on the wild side. Curry paste, cilantro, and lime team up to create layers of Asian flavors.

Seasonal Switch-Up

Fresh produce and nuts join forces in these variations you can enjoy all year long.

SERVES 4 • HANDS-ON TIME: 10 MIN. • TOTAL TIME: 10 MIN.

1 tablespoon peanut oil
½ cup thinly sliced onion
1 teaspoon minced fresh garlic
1½ cups sliced red bell pepper
¼ cup sliced almonds
1 (8.8-ounce) pouch precooked brown rice (such as Uncle Ben's)

1 tablespoon fresh lime juice
2 teaspoons red curry paste (such as Thai Kitchen)
¼ cup cilantro leaves
¼ teaspoon salt
4 lime wedges

❶ Heat a large wok or skillet over medium-high heat. Add oil; swirl to coat. Add onion and garlic; stir-fry 1 minute. Add bell pepper and almonds; stir-fry 2 minutes. Add rice; stir-fry 1 minute. Stir in lime juice, curry paste, cilantro, and salt. Serve with lime wedges.

SERVING SIZE: ¾ cup rice and 1 lime wedge

CALORIES 169; FAT 7.7g (sat 0.8g, mono 3.3g, poly 1.8g); PROTEIN 4g; CARB 23g; FIBER 3g; SUGARS 2g (est. added sugars 0g); CHOL 0mg; IRON 1mg; SODIUM 221mg; CALC 23mg

MUSHROOM & PINE NUT: Heat wok over medium-high heat. Add 1 tablespoon peanut oil; swirl to coat. Add ½ cup sliced onion and 1 teaspoon minced fresh garlic; stir-fry 1 minute. Add 1½ cups sliced cremini mushrooms and ¼ cup pine nuts; stir-fry 2 minutes. Add 1 pouch precooked brown rice; stir-fry 1 minute. Stir in 2 tablespoons balsamic vinegar and ¼ teaspoon salt; cook 1 minute.

SERVES 4 (serving size: ¾ cup) CALORIES 191; FAT 10.6g (sat 1g); SODIUM 158mg

ZUCCHINI & WALNUT: Heat a wok or skillet over medium-high heat. Add 1 tablespoon peanut oil; swirl to coat. Add ½ cup sliced onion and 1 teaspoon minced fresh garlic; stir-fry 1 minute. Add 1½ cups sliced zucchini and ¼ cup chopped walnuts; stir-fry 2 minutes. Add 1 pouch precooked brown rice; stir-fry 1 minute. Stir in 2 tablespoons white wine vinegar, 2 teaspoons Dijon mustard, and ¼ teaspoon salt.

SERVES 4 (serving size: ¾ cup) CALORIES 177; FAT 9.7g (sat 1.1g); SODIUM 191mg

SHAVED SUMMER SQUASH
WITH BASIL, FETA, AND TOMATOES

It's a side. It's a salad. It's an ingenious way to make your vegetable peeler create something besides scraps.

SERVES 8 • HANDS-ON TIME: 10 MIN. • TOTAL TIME: 10 MIN.

3   small yellow squash (about 1 pound)
3   small zucchini (about 1 pound)
2   tablespoons extra-virgin olive oil
1½ tablespoons red wine vinegar
½   teaspoon garlic paste
½   teaspoon salt
¼   teaspoon freshly ground black pepper
1   cup halved grape tomatoes
⅓   cup thinly sliced fresh basil
⅓   cup crumbled feta cheese

1 Shave a very thin layer from yellow squash and zucchini using a vegetable peeler. (Do not peel away color from squash.) Discard peel. Cut squash into ribbons over a large bowl using vegetable peeler; discard seeds.

2 Combine olive oil and next 4 ingredients (through pepper) in a small bowl, stirring with a whisk. Drizzle oil mixture over squash. Add tomatoes, basil, and cheese; toss gently.

SERVING SIZE: ½ cup

CALORIES 63; FAT 5g (sat 1.5g, mono 2.8g, poly 0.6g); PROTEIN 2g; CARB 3g; FIBER 1g; SUGARS 2g (est. added sugars 0g); CHOL 6mg; IRON 2mg; SODIUM 215mg; CALC 42mg

SPICY SESAME-GARLIC SPINACH

A few shakes of soy and rice vinegar add depth and dimension to wilted spinach.

SERVES 4 • HANDS-ON TIME: 8 MIN. • TOTAL TIME: 8 MIN.

1 tablespoon dark sesame oil
¼ teaspoon crushed red pepper
2 garlic cloves, minced
3 (5-ounce) packages fresh baby spinach

2 teaspoons toasted sesame seeds
2 teaspoons lower-sodium soy sauce
1 teaspoon unseasoned rice vinegar

1 Heat a large nonstick skillet over medium-high heat. Add oil to pan; swirl to coat. Add crushed red pepper and garlic to pan; sauté 1 minute. Add one-third of spinach; cook, stirring frequently, 1 minute or just until spinach wilts.

2 Add remaining spinach, one-third at a time. Cook 1 to 2 minutes or just until spinach wilts. Drain spinach through a sieve, pressing lightly with the back of a spoon to remove excess liquid; discard liquid. Transfer spinach to a bowl; stir in sesame seeds, soy sauce, and rice vinegar.

SERVING SIZE: ½ cup

CALORIES 88; FAT 4.3g (sat 0.5g, mono 1.5g, poly 1.5g); PROTEIN 3g; CARB 12g; FIBER 5g; SUGARS 0g (est. added sugars 0g); CHOL 0mg; IRON 4mg; SODIUM 267mg; CALC 81mg

WARM LENTILS
WITH GOAT CHEESE

Using presteamed lentils cuts prep time considerably for this decadent-tasting side.

SERVES 8 • HANDS-ON TIME: 15 MIN. • TOTAL TIME: 25 MIN.

2   teaspoons olive oil
1½ cups finely chopped Vidalia
    or other sweet onion
3   tablespoons water
1   teaspoon chopped fresh thyme
1   garlic clove, minced

2   teaspoons sherry vinegar
¼   teaspoon salt
1   (9-ounce) package refrigerated
    steamed lentils (such as Melissa's)
2   tablespoons crumbled goat cheese
2   tablespoons pine nuts, toasted

① Heat a large nonstick skillet over medium-high heat. Add olive oil to pan; swirl to coat. Add onion; sauté 5 minutes or until tender. Add 3 tablespoons water; cover, reduce heat to medium, and cook 7 minutes or until onion is tender and golden brown, stirring occasionally.

② Add thyme and garlic; sauté 1 minute. Stir in vinegar, salt, and lentils. Cook 2 to 3 minutes or until thoroughly heated, stirring frequently. Remove from heat; sprinkle with goat cheese and pine nuts.

SERVING SIZE: about ½ cup lentils, about 1 teaspoon cheese, and about 1 teaspoon pine nuts

CALORIES 85; FAT 3.5g (sat 0.8g, mono 1.4g, poly 0.9g); PROTEIN 4g; CARB 10g; FIBER 3g; SUGARS 2g (est. added sugars 0g); CHOL 2mg; IRON 1mg; SODIUM 164mg; CALC 26mg

Seasonal Switch-Up

Swapping thyme for parsley, and pine nuts for walnuts might seem subtle, but it gives this side a completely new identity.

NUTTY ALMOND-SESAME RED QUINOA

This one-two protein punch from quinoa and almonds is a favorite on Meatless Monday menus.

SERVES 4 • HANDS-ON TIME: 17 MIN. • TOTAL TIME: 17 MIN.

1⅔ cups water
1   cup red quinoa
¼   cup sliced almonds, toasted
2   tablespoons fresh lemon juice

2   teaspoons olive oil
2   teaspoons dark sesame oil
¼   teaspoon kosher salt
3   green onions, thinly sliced

1 Bring 1⅔ cups water and quinoa to a boil in a medium saucepan. Reduce heat to low, and simmer 12 minutes or until quinoa is tender; drain. Stir in remaining ingredients.

SERVING SIZE: about ½ cup

CALORIES 238; FAT 10g (sat 0.9g, mono 4.4g, poly 1.9g); PROTEIN 8g; CARB 32g; FIBER 3g; SUGARS 3g (est. added sugars 0g); CHOL 0mg; IRON 3mg; SODIUM 132mg; CALC 44mg

Seasonal Switch-Up

Swap out white balsamic for lemon juice and, eighty-six the sesame oil and green onions altogether. Add fresh flat-leaf parsley and halved seedless grapes, and this nutty side becomes a refreshing late-summer salad.

CHARRED BROCCOLI
WITH ORANGE BROWNED BUTTER

Buttery orange flavors elevate broccoli from unsexy side dish to restaurant-quality rock star.

SERVES 4 • HANDS-ON TIME: 10 MIN. • TOTAL TIME: 25 MIN.

10 ounces broccoli florets (2½ cups)
Cooking spray
1 tablespoon butter
1 teaspoon grated orange rind

2 tablespoons fresh orange juice
¼ teaspoon salt
¼ teaspoon freshly ground black pepper

1 Preheat oven to 450°F.

2 Arrange broccoli on a foil-lined baking sheet; coat with cooking spray. Bake at 450°F for 12 minutes or until crisp-tender and lightly browned, stirring once. Heat broiler to high, leaving pan in oven; broil 2 minutes or until lightly charred.

3 Melt butter in a small skillet over medium heat; cook 3 minutes or until browned. Remove from heat. Stir in rind and juice. Combine broccoli and butter mixture in a large bowl. Sprinkle with salt and pepper; toss to coat.

SERVING SIZE: about ⅔ cup

CALORIES 50; **FAT** 3.2g (sat 1.9g, mono 0.8g, poly 0.2g); **PROTEIN** 2g; **CARB** 5g; **FIBER** 2g; **SUGARS** 1g (est. added sugars 0g); **CHOL** 8mg; **IRON** 1mg; **SODIUM** 192mg; **CALC** 37mg

BACON AND CHEDDAR MASHED POTATOES

These mashers are everything you love about the loaded version and a personality-plus complement to a simple chicken breast.

SERVES 6 • HANDS-ON TIME: 10 MIN. • TOTAL TIME: 40 MIN.

2½ pounds Yukon gold or baking potato, peeled and coarsely chopped

½ cup fat-free milk

2 ounces shredded extra-sharp cheddar cheese (about ½ cup)

½ cup fat-free sour cream

½ teaspoon freshly ground black pepper

¼ teaspoon kosher salt

⅓ cup sliced green onions

2 applewood-smoked bacon slices, cooked and finely chopped

1 Place potato in a large saucepan; cover with cold water. Bring to a boil. Reduce heat; simmer 15 minutes or until tender. Drain well; return potato to pan over medium-low heat.

2 Add milk; mash potato mixture with a potato masher to desired consistency. Cook 2 minutes or until thoroughly heated, stirring constantly.

3 Remove from heat. Add cheese, and stir until cheese melts. Stir in sour cream, pepper, and salt. Top with green onions, bacon, and shredded cheddar cheese.

SERVING SIZE: about 1 cup

CALORIES 237; FAT 4.5g (sat 2.5g, mono 1.4g, poly 0.2g); PROTEIN 10g; CARB 38g; FIBER 2g; SUGARS 3g (est. added sugars 0g); CHOL 15mg; IRON 2mg; SODIUM 238mg; CALC 129mg

Eat Now & Later

Mushroom caps make edible bowls for leftover mashed potatoes. Sauté the caps in a little olive oil until tender, stuff with warmed mashed potatoes, and serve.

CRUNCHY ASIAN SLAW

Liven up everything from teriyaki chicken to leftover pork tenderloin when you serve this tangy, slightly spicy slaw.

SERVES 6 • HANDS-ON TIME: 10 MIN. • TOTAL TIME: 10 MIN.

½ cup coarsely chopped unsalted cashews (about 2½ ounces)
¼ cup bottled low-fat sesame-ginger dressing
2 tablespoons fresh lime juice
1 teaspoon fish sauce
1 teaspoon Sriracha (hot chile sauce, such as Huy Fong)
1 teaspoon lemongrass paste
1 small jalapeño, coarsely chopped
½ cup cilantro leaves, chopped
½ cup coarsely chopped fresh mint
¼ cup thinly sliced fresh basil
¼ cup thinly sliced green onions
1 (14-ounce) package cabbage-and-carrot coleslaw

1 Preheat oven to 350°F.

2 Spread cashews in a single layer on a baking sheet. Bake at 350°F for 6 minutes or until lightly toasted. Cool completely.

3 While cashews cool, place dressing and next 5 ingredients (through jalapeño) in a food processor or blender; process until smooth.

4 Combine cashews, cilantro, and remaining ingredients in a large bowl; add dressing, and toss to coat. Serve immediately.

SERVING SIZE: 1 cup

CALORIES 102; **FAT** 6g (sat 0.9g, mono 2.8g, poly 1g); **PROTEIN** 3g; **CARB** 11g; **FIBER** 2g; **SUGARS** 3g (est. added sugars 1g); **CHOL** 0mg; **IRON** 2mg; **SODIUM** 245mg; **CALC** 46mg

Eat Now & Later

Even after a few days in the refrigerator, the cabbage and carrots won't wilt. Stuff this slaw into an Asian wrap, or add it to mu shu wrappers (Chinese pancakes you can find in the frozen section of Asian and specialty markets) for extra texture.

GRILLED CORN
WITH CHIPOTLE-LIME BUTTER

When it comes to corn, the only thing better than topping it with butter and salt is this street cart version bursting with acid and heat.

SERVES 8 • HANDS-ON TIME: 5 MIN. • TOTAL TIME: 20 MIN.

8 small ears shucked yellow corn
Cooking spray
2 tablespoons butter, softened
1 tablespoon finely chopped chipotle chiles, canned in adobo sauce

½ teaspoon grated lime rind
2 teaspoons fresh lime juice
1 garlic clove, crushed
¼ teaspoon salt

1 Preheat grill to medium-high heat.

2 Coat corn with cooking spray, and place on grill rack; grill 13 to 15 minutes or until tender and lightly charred, turning occasionally.

3 While corn cooks, combine butter and next 4 ingredients (through garlic) in a small bowl, stirring until blended.

4 Remove corn from grill, and sprinkle evenly with salt. Serve with butter mixture.

SERVING SIZE: 1 ear of corn and about 1½ teaspoons butter mixture

CALORIES 119; FAT 4.6g (sat 2.2g, mono 1.4g, poly 0.7g); PROTEIN 3g; CARB 20g; FIBER 2g; SUGARS 7g (est. added sugars 0g); CHOL 8mg; IRON 1mg; SODIUM 137mg; CALC 4mg

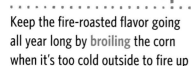

Seasonal Switch-Up

Keep the fire-roasted flavor going all year long by broiling the corn when it's too cold outside to fire up the grill.

HARICOTS VERTS
WITH WARM SHALLOT VINAIGRETTE AND BACON

French green beans get dressed up for parties with this vinaigrette. They can be served at room temp for picnics, too.

SERVES 6 • HANDS-ON TIME: 10 MIN. • TOTAL TIME: 10 MIN.

2   tablespoons olive oil, divided
⅓   cup minced shallots
1   tablespoon sherry vinegar
2   teaspoons Dijon mustard
1   teaspoon maple syrup
⅛   teaspoon salt

¼   teaspoon freshly ground black pepper
2   (8-ounce) packages microwave-in-bag fresh haricots verts (French green beans)
¼   cup cooked crumbled bacon

❶ Heat a small nonstick skillet over medium heat. Add 2 teaspoons oil to pan; swirl to coat. Add shallots; sauté 3 to 4 minutes or until tender but not browned. Transfer to a small bowl; add remaining 4 teaspoons oil, vinegar, and next 4 ingredients (through pepper), stirring with a whisk until blended.

❷ Cook haricots verts according to package directions. Transfer to a serving bowl; drizzle with vinaigrette, and sprinkle with bacon.

SERVING SIZE: about ½ cup

CALORIES 107; FAT 7g (sat 1.5g, mono 4.4g, poly 0.9g); PROTEIN 4g; CARB 7g; FIBER 2g; SUGARS 4g (est. added sugars 1g); CHOL 7mg; IRON 1mg; SODIUM 209mg; CALC 41mg

Savvy Shortcuts

Look for cooked bacon on the grocery store's salad bar to save time. Want it crispier? Pop it in the microwave on a paper towel-lined plate for 30 seconds—just keep an eye on it so it doesn't burn.

ZUCCHINI CAKES
WITH LEMON-DILL SAUCE

Tender yet crispy, these versatile veggie cakes work well with grilled meats or as a main course for a light lunch.

SERVES 6 • HANDS-ON TIME: 22 MIN. • TOTAL TIME: 22 MIN.

1 pound zucchini, shredded (3 cups)
¼ cup lemon pepper-flavored panko (Japanese breadcrumbs)
1 ounce crumbled feta cheese (about ¼ cup)
2 tablespoons all-purpose flour
2 teaspoons chopped fresh dill
½ teaspoon grated lemon rind
¼ teaspoon freshly ground black pepper
1 large egg white, lightly beaten
1 tablespoon canola oil, divided
1 cup plain fat-free Greek yogurt
1 tablespoon fresh lemon juice
1 teaspoon chopped fresh dill
¼ teaspoon kosher salt

1 Preheat oven to 200°F.

2 Line a baking sheet with parchment paper. Firmly squeeze zucchini over a bowl to extract as much water as possible, discarding liquid. Combine zucchini, panko, and next 6 ingredients (through egg white) in a large bowl, stirring well.

3 Heat a large nonstick skillet over medium-high heat. Add 1½ teaspoons oil to pan; swirl to coat. Cook half of batter in 6 (about ¼-cup) portions in hot oil 3 minutes. Carefully turn cakes over; cook 3 minutes or until bottoms are browned. Transfer cooked cakes to prepared baking sheet. Keep warm in oven at 200°F until all cakes are cooked. Repeat procedure with remaining 1½ teaspoons oil and half of batter.

4 Combine yogurt and remaining ingredients in a small bowl, stirring with a whisk. Serve zucchini cakes with yogurt sauce.

SERVING SIZE: 2 zucchini cakes and about 3 tablespoons sauce

CALORIES 99; FAT 4.1g (sat 1.2g, mono 1.8g, poly 0.8g); PROTEIN 6g; CARB 10g; FIBER 1g; SUGARS 3g (est. added sugars 0g); CHOL 6mg; IRON 1mg; SODIUM 233mg; CALC 69mg

SUGAR SNAP PEAS
WITH QUICK-PICKLED RADISHES

Often an afterthought, radishes add a tart and spicy contrast to the sweetness of the snap peas.

SERVES 6 • HANDS-ON TIME: 12 MIN. • TOTAL TIME: 27 MIN.

1   cup thinly sliced radishes
¼   cup red wine vinegar
¼   cup water
2   teaspoons sugar
2   (8-ounce) packages microwave-in-bag fresh sugar snap peas
2   teaspoons rice vinegar
2   teaspoons olive oil
½   teaspoon grated lemon rind
¼   teaspoon kosher salt
⅛   teaspoon freshly ground black pepper
2   tablespoons chopped fresh mint
6   tablespoons crumbled ricotta salata

1 Place radishes in a small bowl. Combine red wine vinegar, ¼ cup water, and sugar, stirring with a whisk until sugar dissolves. Pour over radishes, stirring to coat. Cover and marinate in refrigerator 15 minutes.

2 While radishes marinate, microwave snap peas according to package directions. Plunge peas into ice water; drain. Pat peas dry with a paper towel.

3 Combine rice vinegar and next 4 ingredients (through pepper) in a bowl, stirring with a whisk.

4 Drain radishes, discarding marinade. Combine radishes, snap peas, and mint in a medium bowl; drizzle with vinaigrette, and toss well. Top with crumbled ricotta salata.

SERVING SIZE: ⅔ cup pea mixture and 1 tablespoon cheese

CALORIES 85; **FAT** 4.7g (sat 2.3g, mono 1.1g, poly 0.2g); **PROTEIN** 5g; **CARB** 7g; **FIBER** 2g; **SUGARS** 4g (est. added sugars 0g); **CHOL** 13mg; **IRON** 2mg; **SODIUM** 233mg; **CALC** 60mg

Fast Freeze

Here's a cool trick for extra mint: Stack eight leaves in each section of an ice-cube tray, cover with water, and freeze. Pop them out, and store in a freezer-safe bag; use in ice water, hot or iced tea, soups, and sauces.

BROWNED-BUTTER GNOCCHI
WITH SPINACH AND PINE NUTS

With just a little butter, salt, and pepper, you'll turn vacuum-packed gnocchi dumplings into a sophisticated side.

SERVES 8 • HANDS-ON TIME: 5 MIN. • TOTAL TIME: 5 MIN.

1 (16-ounce) package vacuum-packed gnocchi (such as Vigo)
2 tablespoons butter
2 tablespoons pine nuts
2 garlic cloves, minced
1 (10-ounce) package fresh spinach, torn
¼ teaspoon salt
¼ teaspoon freshly ground black pepper
1 ounce finely shredded Parmesan cheese (about ¼ cup)

1 Cook gnocchi according to package directions, omitting salt and fat; drain.

2 Heat butter in a large nonstick skillet over medium heat. Add pine nuts to pan; cook 3 minutes or until butter and nuts are lightly browned, stirring constantly. Add garlic to pan; cook 1 minute. Add gnocchi and spinach to pan; cook 1 minute or until spinach wilts, stirring constantly. Stir in salt and pepper. Sprinkle with Parmesan cheese.

SERVING SIZE: ½ cup gnocchi mixture and ½ tablespoon cheese

CALORIES 146; FAT 5.6g (sat 2.6g, mono 1.5g, poly 0.9g); PROTEIN 4g; CARB 21g; FIBER 2g; SUGARS 1g (est. added sugars 0g); CHOL 10mg; IRON 1mg; SODIUM 360mg; CALC 89mg

HONEY-GINGER GLAZED CARROTS

This one-pot dish makes a quick and healthy accompaniment to braised pork or seared steak.

SERVES 4 • HANDS-ON TIME: 8 MIN. • TOTAL TIME: 20 MIN.

3   cups (¼-inch-thick) diagonally cut carrot
¼   cup water
2   tablespoons honey
1   tablespoon unsalted butter
2   teaspoons ginger paste
¼   teaspoon salt
½   teaspoon grated lemon rind
⅛   teaspoon freshly ground black pepper

1 Bring first 6 ingredients to a boil in a medium skillet over medium-high heat; reduce heat, cover, and simmer 10 minutes or until carrot is tender. Uncover and cook, stirring frequently, 2 to 3 minutes or until liquid is reduced, syrupy, and coats carrot. Stir in lemon rind and pepper.

SERVING SIZE: ½ cup

CALORIES 102; FAT 3.1g (sat 1.9g, mono 0.8g, poly 0.2g); PROTEIN 1g; CARB 18g; FIBER 3g; SUGARS 14g (est. added sugars 9g); CHOL 8mg; IRON 0mg; SODIUM 239mg; CALC 32mg

ROASTED ASPARAGUS
WITH PECORINO AND PINE NUTS

Just when you thought those tender spears couldn't be more delicious, cheese and nuts work some serious magic to prove you wrong.

SERVES 4 • HANDS-ON TIME: 6 MIN. • TOTAL TIME: 13 MIN.

Eat Now & Later

For a flavorful vegetarian meal, boil pasta noodles according to package directions; drain and return to pot. Add the asparagus mixture, and warm through. Toss with another tablespoon of olive oil, garnish with Parmesan, and serve.

1 pound thin asparagus spears
⅛ teaspoon salt
⅛ teaspoon freshly ground black pepper
1 tablespoon extra-virgin olive oil, divided
1 teaspoon fresh lemon juice
2 tablespoons pine nuts, toasted
2 tablespoons pecorino Romano cheese, shaved

❶ Preheat oven to 450°F.

❷ Snap off tough ends of asparagus. Place asparagus on a rimmed baking sheet; sprinkle with salt and pepper, and drizzle with 2 teaspoons olive oil, tossing to coat. Spread asparagus in a single layer.

❸ Bake at 450°F for 10 minutes or until tender, shaking pan after 5 minutes. Transfer asparagus to a serving platter.

❹ Combine lemon juice and remaining 1 teaspoon olive oil in a small bowl, stirring with a small whisk. Drizzle over asparagus; sprinkle with pine nuts and cheese.

SERVING SIZE: about 3 ounces

CALORIES 87; FAT 7.5g (sat 1.5g, mono 3.6g, poly 2g); PROTEIN 3g; CARB 3g; FIBER 2g; SUGARS 1g (est. added sugars 0g); CHOL 4mg; IRON 2mg; SODIUM 159mg; CALC 46mg

STOVETOP MACARONI AND CHEESE

This rich, creamy homemade mac and cheese comes together in just a few more minutes than the boxed version. Play around with pasta shapes, cheeses, and mix-ins like broccoli, breadcrumbs, or even bacon.

SERVES 6 • HANDS-ON TIME: 11 MIN. • TOTAL TIME: 20 MIN.

5 ounces uncooked elbow macaroni (about 1¼ cups)
1¼ cups 1% low-fat milk, divided
2 tablespoons all-purpose flour
2 ounces sharp cheddar cheese, shredded (½ cup)
1 ounce Gruyère cheese, shredded (about ¼ cup)
¼ teaspoon salt
¼ teaspoon dry mustard
¼ teaspoon freshly ground black pepper

1 Cook pasta according to package directions, omitting salt and fat; drain and keep warm.

2 While pasta cooks, bring 1 cup milk to a boil in a medium saucepan over medium heat, stirring occasionally to prevent scorching. Combine flour and remaining ¼ cup milk in a small bowl, stirring with a whisk until smooth. Gradually add flour mixture to boiling milk, stirring with a whisk. Cook, stirring constantly with a whisk, 3 minutes or until mixture thickens. Remove from heat; add cheeses, salt, mustard, and pepper, whisking until cheese melts. Add cooked pasta, stirring to coat with sauce. Serve immediately.

SERVING SIZE: about ½ cup

CALORIES 179; FAT 5.8g (sat 3.3g, mono 1.6g, poly 0.4g); PROTEIN 9g; CARB 22g; FIBER 1g; SUGARS 3g (est. added sugars 0g); CHOL 18mg; IRON 1mg; SODIUM 215mg; CALC 185mg

Savvy Shortcuts

Here's a "grate" idea: Purchase preshredded cheese to cut your prep time. You can also boil the pasta in advance, refrigerate, and add it in at the end. After adding the pasta, return the pot to medium heat, and warm through before serving.

ROASTED BABY ARTICHOKES
WITH LEMON AIOLI

Don't be scared off by those prickly little leaves. Baby artichokes, bathed in lemon juice and olive oil, can be eaten whole.

SERVES 4 • HANDS-ON TIME: 16 MIN. • TOTAL TIME: 31 MIN.

6 cups water
5 tablespoons fresh lemon juice, divided
12 baby artichokes
5 teaspoons extra-virgin olive oil, divided
¼ teaspoon kosher salt
⅛ teaspoon freshly ground black pepper
¼ cup canola mayonnaise
1 teaspoon minced fresh garlic
½ teaspoon grated lemon rind

1 Preheat oven to 425°F.

2 Combine 6 cups water and ¼ cup juice in a large bowl. Cut off top ½ inch of each artichoke. Cut off stem of each artichoke to within 1 inch of base; peel stem. Remove bottom leaves and tough outer leaves, leaving tender heart and bottom. Cut each artichoke in half lengthwise. Place artichokes in juice mixture.

3 Drain artichokes; pat dry with paper towels. Combine artichokes, 1 tablespoon oil, salt, and pepper; toss well. Arrange in a single layer on a baking sheet. Bake at 425°F for 15 minutes or until tender, turning after 10 minutes.

4 Combine remaining 1 tablespoon juice, remaining 2 teaspoons oil, mayonnaise, garlic, and lemon rind in a small bowl. Serve aioli with artichokes.

SERVING SIZE: 6 artichoke halves and about 1 tablespoon aioli

CALORIES 103; FAT 9.5g (sat 0.7g, mono 6.4g, poly 2g); PROTEIN 1g; CARB 3g; FIBER 1g; SUGARS 1g (est. added sugars 0g); CHOL 5mg; IRON 0mg; SODIUM 241mg; CALC 14mg

FRUITED COUSCOUS
WITH ALMONDS

Expand your carb comfort zone with this sweet and savory couscous. Made of semolina (a type of wheat commonly used in making pasta), couscous is traditionally served in North Africa and the Middle East, and it steams in just minutes.

SERVES 8 • HANDS-ON TIME: 10 MIN. • TOTAL TIME: 10 MIN.

2   teaspoons olive oil
2   tablespoons finely chopped shallots
½   teaspoon turmeric
1⅔ cups fat-free, lower-sodium chicken broth
1½ cups uncooked couscous
¼   cup chopped dried apricots
¼   cup chopped pitted dates
3   tablespoons slivered almonds, toasted
2   tablespoons chopped fresh mint
½   teaspoon grated lemon rind
¼   teaspoon salt

❶ Heat a medium saucepan over medium heat. Add olive oil to pan; swirl to coat. Add shallots; sauté 2 minutes or until tender. Stir in turmeric. Add chicken broth, and bring to a boil; gradually stir in couscous. Remove from heat; cover and let stand 5 minutes. Fluff with a fork.

❷ Stir in apricots and remaining ingredients.

SERVING SIZE: ½ cup

CALORIES 171; FAT 2.6g (sat 0.3g, mono 1.7g, poly 0.5g); PROTEIN 6g; CARB 32g; FIBER 3g; SUGARS 5g; (est. added sugars 0g); CHOL 0mg; IRON 1mg; SODIUM 196mg; CALC 21mg

Seasonal Switch-Up

Use **dried cranberries** instead of **apricots** for a festive dish at turkey time.

CHAPTER 4

CHOP CHOP SALADS

Salads are the supermodels of the table: So many are built upon layers of colorful ingredients, they become almost too beautiful to eat. But add a homemade vinaigrette or ranch dressing, and Couscous Salad Cups, Spinach Salad with Pepper Jelly Vinaigrette, and Curried Quinoa Salad become too hard to resist. This chapter has a salad for every season, because with just a little know-how, the salad days can last all year long.

COUSCOUS SALAD CUPS

Lettuce acts as edible bowls for pearls of couscous. Pair the cups with grilled lamb chops or chicken, or a veggie main with chickpeas and feta.

SERVES 8 • HANDS-ON TIME: 20 MIN. • TOTAL TIME: 20 MIN., INCLUDING DRESSING

Savvy Shortcuts

Buying bottled dressing chops the prep time in half. Find something fruity to add acidity and sweetness to this savory salad.

2 cups organic vegetable broth (such as Swanson Certified Organic)
1 cup uncooked couscous
1 cup matchstick-cut carrot
½ cup chopped green onions
½ cup diced English cucumber
½ cup diced plum tomato
½ cup Pomegranate-Orange Dressing
¼ cup chopped fresh parsley
¼ cup chopped fresh mint
⅛ teaspoon salt
⅛ teaspoon freshly ground black pepper
8 Boston lettuce leaves

1 Bring broth to a boil in a medium saucepan; gradually stir in couscous. Remove from heat; cover, and let stand 5 minutes. Fluff with a fork; cool to room temperature.

2 Combine couscous, carrot, and remaining ingredients except lettuce leaves in a large bowl; toss to combine. Spoon about ⅔ cup couscous mixture into each lettuce leaf.

SERVING SIZE: 1 filled lettuce leaf

CALORIES 135; FAT 2.5g (sat 0.4g, mono 1.7g, poly 0.3g); PROTEIN 3g; CARB 25g; FIBER 2g; SUGARS 4g (est. added sugars 1g); CHOL 0mg; IRON 1mg; SODIUM 237mg; CALC 23mg

POMEGRANATE-ORANGE DRESSING

1 cup fresh orange juice
2½ tablespoons balsamic vinegar
2 tablespoons fresh lemon juice
2 tablespoons pomegranate molasses
2 teaspoons grated orange rind
2 teaspoons minced fresh rosemary
½ teaspoon salt
1 teaspoon brown sugar
½ teaspoon ground cumin
½ teaspoon freshly ground black pepper
¼ teaspoon ground red pepper
4 garlic cloves, minced
¼ cup extra-virgin olive oil

1 Combine all ingredients except oil, stirring with a whisk. Gradually add oil, whisking constantly until well combined. Refrigerate remaining dressing in an airtight container for up to 5 days.

SERVING SIZE: 1 tablespoon (makes 1½ cups)

CALORIES 40; FAT 2.4g (sat 0.3g, mono 1.8g, poly 0.2g); PROTEIN 0g; CARB 4g; FIBER 0g; SUGARS 3g (est. added sugars 1g); CHOL 0mg; IRON 0mg; SODIUM 99mg; CALC 8mg

MULTIBEAN SALAD

Edamame packs potassium into this updated three-bean salad. Throw in some tofu and make it a hearty vegetarian lunch, or serve this colorful salad as a side at a backyard barbecue.

SERVES 6 • HANDS-ON TIME: 15 MIN. • TOTAL TIME: 15 MIN.

2 cups (½-inch-thick) diagonally cut haricots verts (French green beans; about 8 ounces)

2 cups (½-inch-thick) diagonally cut wax beans (about 8 ounces)

1 cup frozen shelled edamame (green soybeans)

1 cup grape or cherry tomatoes, halved

½ cup finely chopped orange bell pepper

½ cup thinly sliced red onion

2 tablespoons sherry vinegar

½ teaspoon sugar

¼ teaspoon Dijon mustard

2 teaspoons extra-virgin olive oil

¼ cup chopped fresh parsley

¼ teaspoon salt

¼ teaspoon freshly ground black pepper

1 Steam haricots verts, wax beans, and edamame, covered, 6 minutes or until haricots verts and wax beans are crisp-tender. Drain and plunge beans into ice water; drain. Combine beans, tomatoes, bell pepper, and onion in a large bowl.

2 Combine vinegar, sugar, and mustard, stirring with a whisk. Gradually add oil to vinegar mixture, stirring constantly with a whisk. Stir in parsley, salt, and black pepper. Drizzle vinaigrette over bean mixture; toss gently to coat.

SERVING SIZE: about 1 cup

CALORIES 89; FAT 2.7g (sat 0.2g, mono 1.2g, poly 0.2g); PROTEIN 4g; CARB 11g; FIBER 4g; SUGARS 4g (est. added sugars 0g); CHOL 0mg; IRON 2mg; SODIUM 117mg; CALC 57mg

TABBOULEH
WITH CHICKEN AND RED PEPPER

Leftover or rotisserie chicken turns this salad into a main dish with lemony hummus and spicy whole-wheat pita chips on the side. This make-ahead meal works best when the cucumber and tomato are stored separately.

SERVES 4 • HANDS-ON TIME: 20 MIN. • TOTAL TIME: 45 MIN., INCLUDING CHILL TIME

½ cup uncooked bulgur
½ cup boiling water
1½ cups diced plum tomato
¾ cup shredded skinless, boneless rotisserie chicken breast
¾ cup minced fresh flat-leaf parsley
½ cup finely chopped red bell pepper

½ cup diced English cucumber
¼ cup minced fresh mint
1½ tablespoons fresh lemon juice
1 tablespoon extra-virgin olive oil
½ teaspoon salt
¼ teaspoon freshly ground black pepper

1 Combine bulgur and ½ cup boiling water in a large bowl. Cover and let stand 15 minutes or until bulgur is tender. Drain well; return bulgur to bowl. Cool to room temperature.

2 Add tomato and remaining ingredients; toss well.

SERVING SIZE: 1¼ cups

CALORIES 161; FAT 5g (sat 0.9g, mono 3.1g, poly 0.7g); PROTEIN 12g; CARB 19g; FIBER 5g; SUGARS 3g (est. added sugars 0g); CHOL 22mg; IRON 2mg; SODIUM 325mg; CALC 41mg

SPINACH SALAD
WITH PEPPER JELLY VINAIGRETTE

Mixing jelly into vinaigrette adds sweetness and snap to salads. Make it ahead, and refrigerate; then bring to room temperature before tossing with the spinach.

SERVES 6 • HANDS-ON TIME: 5 MIN. • TOTAL TIME: 25 MIN., INCLUDING CHILL TIME

¼ cup red pepper jelly
2 tablespoons cider vinegar
1 tablespoon extra-virgin olive oil
⅛ teaspoon kosher salt
⅛ teaspoon freshly ground black pepper

8 cups fresh baby spinach
1 ounce crumbled Gorgonzola cheese (about ¼ cup)
¼ cup dry-roasted pistachios

1 Place jelly in a 1-cup glass measure. Microwave at HIGH 30 seconds. Add vinegar, oil, salt, and pepper, stirring with a whisk until blended. Cool to room temperature.

2 Combine spinach and cheese in a large bowl. Drizzle vinegar mixture over spinach mixture; toss well. Sprinkle with nuts. Serve immediately.

SERVING SIZE: 1 cup spinach mixture and 2 teaspoons nuts

CALORIES 99; FAT 6g (sat 1.6g, mono 2.9g, poly 1g); PROTEIN 3g; CARB 10g; FIBER 2g; SUGARS 2g (est. added sugars 0g); CHOL 4mg; IRON 1mg; SODIUM 196mg; CALC 54mg

Seasonal Switch-Up

In winter, when fresh spinach is hard to find, kale is a vitamin-packed substitute that stands up to the pepper jelly vinaigrette and Gorgonzola. Wash it right before use, cut the greens away from the rib, and tear into small pieces.

SHAVED ASPARAGUS
WITH MANCHEGO AND ALMONDS

Select medium or thick asparagus. Hold the tough stem of the stalk in your fingers, and use a sharp peeler to peel toward the head at the tender part. Can't find walnut oil? Substitute 1½ teaspoons extra-virgin olive oil. Serve with grilled whole-grain bread for a light lunch.

SERVES 4 • HANDS-ON TIME: 23 MIN. • TOTAL TIME: 23 MIN.

1½ tablespoons extra-virgin olive oil
2 teaspoons sherry vinegar
1½ teaspoons walnut oil
1 teaspoon minced fresh garlic
¼ teaspoon salt
¼ teaspoon freshly ground black pepper
1 pound large asparagus spears
1 tablespoon chopped fresh flat-leaf parsley

8 cups water
2 tablespoons white vinegar
4 large eggs
2 tablespoons slivered almonds, toasted
1 ounce Manchego cheese, shaved (about ¼ cup)

1 Combine first 6 ingredients in a large bowl, stirring with a whisk. Using a sharp peeler, thinly peel asparagus to equal 3 cups asparagus ribbons. Add asparagus and parsley to bowl; toss gently to coat.

2 Combine 8 cups water and white vinegar in a large skillet; bring to a simmer. Break each egg into a custard cup, and pour each gently into pan. Cook 3 minutes or until desired degree of doneness. Remove eggs from pan using a slotted spoon.

3 Place asparagus mixture on each of 4 plates. Top each serving with almonds, egg, and cheese.

SERVING SIZE: ⅔ cup asparagus mixture, 1½ teaspoons almonds, 1 egg, and 1 tablespoon cheese
CALORIES 207; FAT 16.4g (sat 4.4g, mono 8.3g, poly 2.3g); PROTEIN 11g; CARB 5g; FIBER 2g; SUGARS 2g (est. added sugars 0g); CHOL 194mg; IRON 3mg; SODIUM 279mg; CALC 154mg

CREAMY BLUEBERRY CHICKEN SALAD

This chicken salad gets a big antioxidant boost from fresh blueberries. Toss them gently with the Greek yogurt and chicken, being careful not to damage their delicate flesh. Steer clear of frozen blueberries when fresh are out of season—even when thawed, they can water down the mix.

SERVES 6 • HANDS-ON TIME: 15 MIN. • TOTAL TIME: 15 MIN.

½ cup thinly vertically sliced red onion
⅓ cup diced celery
¼ cup torn fresh basil
12 ounces shredded skinless, boneless rotisserie chicken breast (about 3 cups)
½ teaspoon kosher salt, divided

½ cup plain 2% reduced-fat Greek yogurt
2½ tablespoons fresh lemon juice, divided
1 tablespoon honey
2 cups fresh blueberries
1 (5-ounce) package baby arugula
2 teaspoons extra-virgin olive oil
¼ teaspoon freshly ground black pepper

1 Combine first 4 ingredients in a medium bowl; sprinkle with ¼ teaspoon salt. Combine yogurt, 1 tablespoon lemon juice, and honey in a small bowl, stirring with a whisk. Add yogurt mixture to chicken mixture; toss to coat. Gently stir in blueberries. Place remaining 1½ tablespoons lemon juice, remaining ¼ teaspoon salt, arugula, oil, and pepper in a bowl; toss to coat. Divide arugula mixture evenly among 6 plates; top each serving with about ¾ cup chicken mixture.

SERVING SIZE: about ¾ cup

CALORIES 188; FAT 8.5g (sat 2.1g, mono 3.9g, poly 1.3g); PROTEIN 16g; CARB 13g; FIBER 2g; SUGARS 10g (est. added sugars 3g); CHOL 75mg; IRON 1mg; SODIUM 369mg; CALC 69mg

SOBA NOODLE SALAD
WITH CITRUS VINAIGRETTE

Often labeled as buckwheat noodles, soba can be found in the Asian section of most supermarkets. It cooks a little quicker than regular pasta and adds an earthy flavor to this salad that's equal parts sweet and savory.

SERVES 4 • HANDS-ON TIME: 10 MIN. • TOTAL TIME: 12 MIN.

1   (8-ounce) package soba noodles
1¼ cups frozen shelled edamame
    (green soybeans)
¾   cup matchstick-cut carrots
⅓   cup sliced green onions
2   tablespoons chopped fresh cilantro
1½ teaspoons chopped serrano chile
1   pound peeled and deveined
    medium shrimp
¼   teaspoon salt
¼   teaspoon freshly ground black pepper
Cooking spray
2   tablespoons fresh orange juice
2   tablespoons fresh lime juice
1   tablespoon lower-sodium soy sauce
1   tablespoon dark sesame oil
1   tablespoon olive oil

1 Cook noodles in boiling water 7 minutes or until almost al dente. Add edamame to pan; cook 1 minute or until thoroughly heated. Drain. Place noodle mixture in a large bowl. Add carrots, onions, cilantro, and chile; toss.

2 Heat a large skillet over medium-high heat. Sprinkle shrimp with salt and pepper. Coat pan with cooking spray. Add shrimp; cook 1½ minutes on each side. Add shrimp to noodle mixture.

3 Combine orange juice and remaining ingredients in a bowl, stirring well with a whisk. Drizzle juice mixture over noodle mixture; toss well.

SERVING SIZE: about 2 cups

CALORIES 411; FAT 7.2g (sat 0.6g, mono 2.6g, poly 0.6g); PROTEIN 38g; CARB 53g; FIBER 3g; SUGARS 3g (est. added sugars 0g); CHOL 183mg; IRON 3mg; SODIUM 573mg; CALC 119mg

Eat Now & Later

Bake a chicken breast with a little soy sauce, chop, and add to the top of this salad for lunch the next day. Eat it with chopsticks, and finish it off with a fortune cookie.

HEIRLOOM TOMATO PANZANELLA

Bumper crop of tomatoes? Put summer's bounty to work alongside grilled corn and red onions. What a great way to give day-old bread a second life.

SERVES 6 • HANDS-ON TIME: 40 MIN. • TOTAL TIME: 45 MIN.

3   tablespoons olive oil
2   tablespoons red wine vinegar
¼   teaspoon salt
⅛   teaspoon freshly ground black pepper
1   small garlic clove, minced
2   ears shucked corn
1   (9-ounce) red onion, cut into
    6 wedges

Cooking spray
2   (2-ounce) slices Italian bread
    (1-inch thick)
4   cups coarsely chopped
    heirloom tomatoes
⅓   cup basil leaves, cut into thin strips

1. Preheat grill to medium-high heat.

2. Combine first 5 ingredients in a small bowl, stirring with a whisk.

3. Place corn and red onion on grill rack coated with cooking spray; grill 13 minutes or until corn is charred and onion is tender, turning corn frequently, and onion after 7 minutes. Add bread to grill rack after 9 minutes; grill 2 minutes on each side or until toasted.

4. Cut kernels from ears of corn; coarsely chop onion. Tear bread into 1½-inch pieces. Combine tomatoes, basil, corn kernels, onion, and bread in a large bowl. Drizzle with vinaigrette; toss well.

SERVING SIZE: 1⅓ cups

CALORIES 185; FAT 7.8g (sat 1.2g, mono 5.3g, poly 1.1g); PROTEIN 5g; CARB 27g; FIBER 4g; SUGARS 8g (est. added sugars 0g); CHOL 0mg; IRON 1mg; SODIUM 245mg; CALC 28mg

CANDIED WALNUT, PEAR, AND LEAFY GREEN SALAD

Sugared walnuts give this salad top-notch taste and texture. Make a double batch for a sweet snack or just-because gift.

SERVES 8 • HANDS-ON TIME: 15 MIN. • TOTAL TIME: 15 MIN.

⅓ cup sugar
⅔ cup chopped walnuts, toasted
Cooking spray
½ teaspoon kosher salt, divided
2 tablespoons white balsamic vinegar
1½ teaspoons Dijon mustard
3 tablespoons extra-virgin olive oil

1 tablespoon capers, drained and chopped
4 cups torn green leaf lettuce
4 cups chopped romaine lettuce
4 cups chopped radicchio
1 ripe red Anjou pear, thinly sliced
¼ teaspoon freshly ground black pepper

1 Place sugar in a small heavy saucepan over medium-high heat; cook until sugar dissolves, stirring gently as needed to dissolve sugar evenly (about 1 minute). Continue cooking 1 minute or until golden. (Do not stir.) Remove from heat; carefully stir in nuts to coat evenly. Spread nuts on a baking sheet coated with cooking spray; separate nuts quickly. Sprinkle with ¼ teaspoon salt. Cool; break into small pieces.

2 Combine vinegar and mustard, stirring with a whisk. Gradually add oil, stirring constantly with a whisk. Stir in capers.

3 Combine lettuces and radicchio; top with pear and candied walnuts. Drizzle dressing evenly over salad; sprinkle with remaining ¼ teaspoon salt and pepper. Toss gently to combine.

SERVING SIZE: about 1 cup

CALORIES 169; FAT 11.6g (sat 1.3g, mono 4.6g, poly 5.2g); PROTEIN 2g; CARB 16g; FIBER 2g; SUGARS 12g (est. added sugars 8g); CHOL 0mg; IRON 1mg; SODIUM 204mg; CALC 32mg

CURRIED QUINOA SALAD
WITH CUCUMBER-MINT RAITA

Full of Indian flavors, this salad features quinoa, a high-protein grain that cooks quickly. Stick with the Madras curry for a nice heat that's balanced out by the raita, or switch to regular curry powder for something more subtle.

SERVES 6 • HANDS-ON TIME: 12 MIN. • TOTAL TIME: 40 MIN., INCLUDING CHILL TIME

1   teaspoon olive oil
2   teaspoons Madras curry powder
1   garlic clove, crushed
1   cup uncooked quinoa
2   cups water
½   teaspoon kosher salt
1   diced peeled ripe mango
½   cup diced celery
¼   cup thinly sliced green onions
3   tablespoons chopped fresh cilantro
3   tablespoons currants
¼   cup finely diced peeled English cucumber
2   teaspoons chopped fresh mint
1   (6-ounce) carton plain low-fat yogurt
1   (6-ounce) package fresh baby spinach

Eat Now & Later

Stuff a warm pita full of this salad for a filling lunch, or line a tortilla with hummus, scoop several spoonfuls on top, and make it a wrap.

① Heat a medium saucepan over medium-high heat. Add oil to pan; swirl to coat. Add curry powder and garlic to pan; cook 1 minute, stirring constantly. Add quinoa and 2 cups water; bring to a boil. Cover, reduce heat, and simmer 16 minutes or until tender. Remove from heat; stir in salt. Cool completely.

② Add mango and next 4 ingredients (through currants) to cooled quinoa; toss gently.

③ Combine cucumber, mint, and yogurt in a small bowl; stir well. Place spinach on each of 6 plates; top each serving with quinoa mixture and raita.

SERVING SIZE: about ¾ cup spinach, ¾ cup quinoa, and about 2 tablespoons raita

CALORIES 177; FAT 3.4g (sat 0.7g, mono 1.3g, poly 1.2g); PROTEIN 7g; CARB 31g; FIBER 4g; SUGARS 10g (est. added sugars 2g); CHOL 2mg; IRON 3mg; SODIUM 212mg; CALC 111mg

SESAME-CARROT EDAMAME SALAD

An awesome Asian salad that straddles all seasons, this dish can be made in advance to let the flavors meld. Pair it with stir-fry, Asian pork tacos topped with cabbage slaw, or the Teriyaki Pork Tenderloin Mu Shu Wraps on page 61.

SERVES 4 • HANDS-ON TIME: 5 MIN. • TOTAL TIME: 8 MIN.

8   cups water
1½ cups frozen shelled edamame
    (green soybeans)
2   tablespoons chopped fresh cilantro
1½ tablespoons rice vinegar

1½ tablespoons dark sesame oil
½   teaspoon sesame seeds
¼   teaspoon kosher salt
1   cup shredded carrot
¼   cup sliced green onions

1 Bring 8 cups water to a boil in a saucepan. Add edamame; cook 3 minutes or until tender. Drain.

2 Combine cilantro, vinegar, sesame oil, sesame seeds, and salt in a medium bowl, stirring with a whisk. Stir in edamame, carrot, and green onions.

SERVING SIZE: ½ cup

CALORIES 109; FAT 7.5g (sat 0.8g, mono 2.1g, poly 2.3g); PROTEIN 5g; CARB 7g; FIBER 3g; SUGARS 3g (est. added sugars 0g); CHOL 0mg; IRON 1mg; SODIUM 143mg; CALC 44mg

BEET CARPACCIO SALAD

Paper thin-sliced colorful beets are the star ingredient of this salad with arugula, orange sections, feta cheese, and candied almonds.

SERVES 6 • HANDS-ON TIME: 15 MIN. • TOTAL TIME: 15 MIN.

1 navel orange
2 tablespoons olive oil
1½ tablespoons rice vinegar
1 teaspoon honey
½ teaspoon Dijon mustard
¼ teaspoon salt
⅛ teaspoon freshly ground pepper

6 ounces peeled small yellow beets
6 ounces peeled small candy cane (Chioggia) beets
½ cup crumbled feta cheese
¼ cup candied almond pieces
3 cups arugula

1 Grate rind from orange to measure ½ teaspoon; place in a small bowl. Peel and section orange over another bowl; squeeze membranes to extract juice. Reserve 1 tablespoon juice; add to orange rind. Coarsely chop orange sections to measure ½ cup; set aside. Add oil and next 5 ingredients (through pepper) to orange rind mixture, stirring with a whisk.

2 Thinly slice beets to measure 1 cup each using a mandoline. Combine yellow beets and 2 tablespoons vinaigrette in a medium bowl; toss well. Layer yellow beet slices on a platter. Combine candy cane beet slices and 2 tablespoons vinaigrette in same medium bowl; toss well. Layer candy cane beet slices on top of yellow beet slices.

3 Top beet slices with reserved ½ cup chopped orange sections. Sprinkle with feta cheese and almond pieces.

4 Combine arugula and remaining 1 tablespoon vinaigrette in a medium bowl; toss gently. Top salad with arugula.

SERVING SIZE: ⅙th of salad

CALORIES 135; FAT 9.5g (sat 2.7g, mono 5.3g, poly 1.2g); PROTEIN 4g; CARB 10g; FIBER 2g; SUGARS 7g (est. added sugars 1g); CHOL 11mg; IRON 1mg; SODIUM 274mg; CALC 106mg

BROWN RICE AND QUINOA TEX-MEX SALAD

This hearty, whole grain–filled salad is delicious for dinner and even better at lunch the next day. Allowing the beans and grains to marinate overnight makes it even more flavorful. But keep your greens and your bean-and-grain mixture separate so the greens stay fresh and crunchy.

SERVES 4 • HANDS-ON TIME: 15 MIN. • TOTAL TIME: 25 MIN.

1   (8.5-ounce) package ready-to-heat quinoa and brown rice pilaf with garlic
⅓   cup refrigerated lemon vinaigrette
2   tablespoons finely chopped green onions
1   tablespoon fresh lime juice
1   tablespoon ground cumin
2   cups grape tomato, halved
1   cup fresh corn kernels

½   cup chopped fresh cilantro
¼   cup chopped red onion
1   (15-ounce) can unsalted black beans, rinsed and drained
1   (15-ounce) can reduced-sodium Great Northern beans, rinsed and drained
10 cups chopped romaine lettuce
6   tablespoons unsalted pumpkinseed kernels, toasted

❶ Prepare pilaf according to package directions. Spread on a large plate; cool 5 minutes.

❷ Combine vinaigrette and next 3 ingredients (through cumin) in a small bowl, stirring with a whisk. Place pilaf, grape tomato halves, and next 5 ingredients (through Great Northern beans) in a large bowl; drizzle with vinaigrette, and toss well. Let stand 10 minutes.

❸ Divide lettuce evenly among 6 bowls; top evenly with bean salad and pumpkinseed kernels.

SERVING SIZE: 1⅔ cups romaine, 1¼ cups bean salad, and 1 tablespoon pumpkinseed kernels

CALORIES 457; FAT 14.9g (sat 2.1g, mono 1.9g, poly 2.7g); PROTEIN 19g; CARB 66g; FIBER 14g; SUGARS 10g (est. added sugars 0g); CHOL 0mg; IRON 12mg; SODIUM 430mg; CALC 140mg

Eat Now & Later

From salad to burrito in seconds: Fill an oversized tortilla with the mixture, add ½ cup rotisserie chicken, wrap, heat, and eat.

CRUNCHY AUTUMN SALAD

Sliced Brussels sprouts add crunch to this salad, with a hint of sweetness from fresh apple and dried cranberries. Serve it alongside short ribs braised with onion, carrot, and celery, and a cold beer.

SERVES 7 • HANDS-ON TIME: 7 MIN. • TOTAL TIME: 7 MIN.

3   cups thinly sliced Brussels sprouts
3   cups bagged prewashed baby kale
2   cups bagged broccoli coleslaw
1¾ cups (½-inch) diced Fuji or
    Granny Smith apple
⅓ cup sweetened dried cranberries

3   tablespoons unsalted pumpkinseed
    kernels, toasted
½   cup fat-free poppy seed dressing
2   tablespoons fresh lemon juice
⅛   teaspoon salt
⅛   teaspoon freshly ground black pepper

1 Combine first 6 ingredients in a large bowl. Combine poppy seed dressing and lemon juice in a small bowl, stirring with a whisk. Add to salad; toss to coat. Sprinkle with salt and pepper; toss well.

SERVING SIZE: 1½ cups

CALORIES 109; FAT 1.9g (sat 0.3g, mono 0.5g, poly 0.8g); PROTEIN 3g; CARB 22g; FIBER 4g; SUGARS 11g
(est. added sugars 2g); CHOL 0mg; IRON 1mg; SODIUM 144mg; CALC 45mg

STEAK, PEAR, AND WATERCRESS SALAD

This flavorful salad puts protein, vegetables, and fruit on one plate. Switch it up and grill the steaks, or pan-cook them for a quick weeknight meal.

SERVES 4 • HANDS-ON TIME: 13 MIN. • TOTAL TIME: 18 MIN.

2½ tablespoons extra-virgin olive oil, divided
1 (12-ounce) flank steak, trimmed
¾ teaspoon salt, divided
½ teaspoon freshly ground black pepper
2 tablespoons sherry vinegar

1 small shallot, chopped
2 (4-ounce) packages watercress
½ cup thinly sliced red onion
1 peeled ripe pear, thinly sliced
2 tablespoons crumbled blue cheese

1 Heat a large skillet over medium-high heat. Add 1½ teaspoons oil to pan; swirl to coat. Sprinkle steak with ½ teaspoon salt and pepper. Add steak to pan; cook 4 minutes on each side or until desired degree of doneness. Place steak on a cutting board; let stand 5 minutes. Cut across grain into thin slices.

2 Place remaining 2 tablespoons oil, remaining ¼ teaspoon salt, vinegar, and shallot in a mini food processor; pulse until mixture is almost smooth.

3 Arrange one-fourth of watercress on each of 4 plates. Top watercress evenly with onion and pear; sprinkle with cheese. Divide steak evenly among salads; drizzle vinaigrette over each serving.

SERVING SIZE: 1½ cups

CALORIES 255; FAT 14.4g (sat 3.7g, mono 8.2g, poly 1.1g); PROTEIN 21g; CARB 10g; FIBER 2g; SUGARS 5g (est. added sugars 0g); CHOL 56mg; IRON 2mg; SODIUM 573mg; CALC 119mg

ROASTED FENNEL– CITRUS SALAD

"Winter salad" is not an oxymoron. Roasting the fennel here coaxes out its natural sweetness, which works well with the citrus and pistachios. Who says all the good stuff is gone when it's cold outside?

SERVES 6 • HANDS-ON TIME: 25 MIN. • TOTAL TIME: 25 MIN.

2 cups thinly sliced fennel bulb (about 1 medium bulb)
1 cup thinly vertically sliced red onion
Cooking spray
¼ teaspoon kosher salt
⅛ teaspoon freshly ground black pepper
1½ tablespoons olive oil
1 tablespoon white balsamic vinegar
¼ teaspoon grated orange rind
1 cup orange sections (3 medium oranges)
¼ cup chopped pistachios
1 ounce fresh pecorino Romano cheese, shaved (about ¼ cup)

① Preheat oven to 400°F.

② Place fennel and red onion on a rimmed baking sheet lightly coated with cooking spray. Coat vegetables with cooking spray. Sprinkle with salt and pepper. Bake at 400°F for 15 minutes or until fennel and onion are tender and golden. Cool slightly.

③ Combine olive oil, vinegar, and orange rind in a small bowl, stirring with a whisk.

④ Arrange orange sections, fennel, and red onion on a serving platter. Drizzle with vinaigrette. Sprinkle with pistachios and cheese.

SERVING SIZE: ⅙th of salad

CALORIES 112; FAT 7.5g (sat 1.7g, mono 4.3g, poly 1.2g); PROTEIN 3g; CARB 9g; FIBER 2g; SUGARS 5g (est. added sugars 0g); CHOL 5mg; IRON 0mg; SODIUM 211mg; CALC 74mg

CRAB AND HEIRLOOM TOMATO SALAD

This is the textbook definition of easy entertaining. In less than 15 minutes, you can create a salad full of crabmeat, cilantro, bell peppers, and jalapeño perfectly paired with fresh tomatoes. Though it's tempting to make this recipe your year-round go-to, file it away for summer when tomatoes are at their peak.

SERVES 4 • HANDS-ON TIME: 14 MIN. • TOTAL TIME: 14 MIN.

⅓ cup cilantro leaves
4 mini sweet bell peppers, thinly diagonally sliced
1 large shallot, thinly sliced
1 jalapeño pepper, thinly diagonally sliced
12 ounces jumbo lump crabmeat, shell pieces removed
2½ tablespoons canola mayonnaise
1 teaspoon grated lime rind
1 tablespoon fresh lime juice
2 pounds heirloom tomatoes, sliced
1½ tablespoons extra-virgin olive oil
¼ teaspoon kosher salt
¼ teaspoon freshly ground black pepper
¼ cup small basil leaves

1 Combine first 5 ingredients in a large bowl. Combine mayonnaise, rind, and juice in a small bowl, stirring with a whisk. Add mayonnaise mixture to crab mixture; toss gently to coat. Arrange tomatoes on a serving platter; drizzle with oil. Sprinkle tomatoes with salt and pepper. Mound crab mixture over tomatoes. Sprinkle with basil leaves.

SERVING SIZE: about 1 cup tomato and ¾ cup crab mixture

CALORIES 200; **FAT** 8.6g (sat 1g, mono 5.3g, poly 1.9g); **PROTEIN** 18g; **CARB** 13g; **FIBER** 4g; **SUGARS** 8g (est. added sugars 0g); **CHOL** 83mg; **IRON** 1mg; **SODIUM** 536mg; **CALC** 109mg

SIMPLE AVOCADO SALAD

Often called "nature's mayonnaise," avocado adds creaminess without any cream or cheese. Serve this salad as a light complement to burritos, enchiladas, or fajitas in place of guacamole.

SERVES 4 • HANDS-ON TIME: 10 MIN. • TOTAL TIME: 10 MIN.

2   tablespoons chopped red onion
1½ tablespoons fresh lime juice
1½ tablespoons extra-virgin olive oil
1   large diced peeled ripe avocado

4   cups baby arugula
¼   teaspoon salt
¼   teaspoon freshly ground black pepper

1 Combine onion, lime juice, and olive oil in a small bowl, stirring with a whisk. Add avocado; toss gently to combine. Divide arugula among 4 salad plates; top evenly with avocado mixture. Sprinkle evenly with salt and pepper.

SERVING SIZE: 1½ cups

CALORIES 134; FAT 12.6g (sat 1.8g, mono 8.6g, poly 1.5g); PROTEIN 2g; CARB 6g; FIBER 4g; SUGARS 1g (est. added sugars 0g); CHOL 0mg; IRON 1mg; SODIUM 155mg; CALC 41mg

Savvy Shortcuts

Remove the avocado pit like a pro: Cut the avocado in half, and twist the two sides apart. Hold the side with the pit in one hand, and with one gentle motion, bury the knife in the pit with the other. Give the knife a little twist, and the pit will pop right out.

SMOKED SALMON AND WHEAT BERRY SALAD

Inspired by the lox bagel, this whole-grain salad is brimming with capers, red onion, dill, and cold-smoked salmon. Wheat berries are the wheat grain stripped of its outer hull—they can take nearly an hour to cook, so make a big batch and refrigerate what you don't need for another recipe later in the week.

SERVES 4 • HANDS-ON TIME: 13 MIN. • TOTAL TIME: 13 MIN.

Eat Now & Later

Dip for lunch? Why not? Scoop up the salmon-wheat berry mixture with baked bagel chips.

3   tablespoons water
2   tablespoons capers, drained
2   tablespoons plain 2% reduced-fat Greek yogurt
2   tablespoons cider vinegar
1   teaspoon Dijon mustard
¾   teaspoon freshly ground black pepper
½   teaspoon sugar

3   ounces ⅓-less-fat cream cheese
2   cups cooked wheat berries
1½ cups thinly sliced English cucumber
¾   cup thinly vertically sliced red onion
⅓   cup fresh dill
3½ ounces cold-smoked salmon, cut into thin strips, divided
4   cups baby spinach leaves

1 Combine first 8 ingredients in a bowl, stirring well with a whisk. Stir in wheat berries, cucumber, onion, dill, and 1½ ounces salmon; toss to coat. Place spinach in each of 4 bowls; top each serving with wheat berry mixture and remaining salmon.

SERVING SIZE: 1 cup spinach, 1 cup wheat berry mixture, and ½ ounce salmon

CALORIES 275; FAT 7.1g (sat 3g, mono 1.3g, poly 0.6g); PROTEIN 15g; CARB 41g; FIBER 7g; SUGARS 4g (est. added sugars 1g); CHOL 29mg; IRON 1mg; SODIUM 581mg; CALC 87mg

ROASTED TOMATO, HARICOTS VERTS, AND OLIVE SALAD

Full of Mediterranean flavors, this salad gets its slight sweetness from caramelized vegetables. Serve it as a side or with seared tuna and steamed new potatoes for a full meal.

SERVES 6 • HANDS-ON TIME: 10 MIN. • TOTAL TIME: 22 MIN.

2   (8-ounce) packages haricots verts (French green beans)
2   tablespoons olive oil, divided
¼   teaspoon kosher salt
¼   teaspoon freshly ground black pepper, divided

2   cups grape tomatoes
2   small shallots, thinly sliced
Cooking spray
⅓   cup pitted kalamata olives, halved
1   tablespoon white balsamic vinegar

1. Preheat oven to 425°F.
2. Place a large rimmed baking sheet in preheated oven for 5 minutes.
3. Combine beans, 1 tablespoon olive oil, salt, and ⅛ teaspoon pepper in a large bowl, tossing to coat. Spread beans in a single layer on preheated baking sheet. Bake at 425°F for 12 minutes or until tender.
4. While beans cook, place tomatoes on 1 side of a parchment paper–lined rimmed baking sheet. Place shallots on opposite side of baking sheet. Lightly coat vegetables with cooking spray; sprinkle with remaining ⅛ teaspoon pepper.
5. Place baking sheet on same rack in oven as beans, and bake at 425°F for 12 minutes or until tomatoes pop and shallots are golden.
6. Combine olives, beans, tomatoes, and shallots in a large bowl. Drizzle with remaining 1 tablespoon olive oil and balsamic vinegar; toss well. Serve warm or chilled.

SERVING SIZE: 1 cup salad

CALORIES 113; FAT 7g (sat 0.9g, mono 5.1g, poly 0.8g); PROTEIN 3g; CARB 11g; FIBER 3g; SUGARS 5g (est. added sugars 0g); CHOL 0mg; IRON 5mg; SODIUM 211mg; CALC 42mg

Eat Now & Later

Use your noodles: A small bowl of penne or rotini turns this salad into a perfect lunch portion of pasta salad. Sprinkle with Parmesan, and enjoy it hot or cold.

MEDITERRANEAN CHICKPEA SALAD

This summertime salad is full of bold flavors and colors. Garnish with baked pita chips, or crush them up for extra texture.

SERVES 4 • HANDS-ON TIME: 10 MIN. • TOTAL TIME: 10 MIN.

Savvy Shortcuts

Find a fresh, healthy citrus vinaigrette at the store and shave a few minutes off the prep time. Look for one that has about 170 calories or less and no more than 2g saturated fat and 200mg of sodium per serving (generally 2 tablespoons).

3 tablespoons fresh lemon juice
3 tablespoons olive oil
½ teaspoon Dijon mustard
½ teaspoon honey
¼ teaspoon grated lemon rind
¼ teaspoon salt
⅛ teaspoon freshly ground black pepper
4 cups bagged baby spinach blend with radicchio, coarsely chopped

1 cup grape tomatoes, halved
2 ounces crumbled feta cheese (about ½ cup)
⅓ cup finely chopped red onion
¼ cup fresh flat-leaf parsley
2 (15½-ounce) cans lower-sodium chickpeas (garbanzo beans), rinsed and drained

1 Combine first 7 ingredients in a large bowl, stirring with a whisk. Add greens and remaining ingredients; toss well.

SERVING SIZE: 1⅔ cups salad

CALORIES 300; FAT 17.1g (sat 4.5g, mono 8.9g, poly 2.5g); PROTEIN 11g; CARB 28g; FIBER 8g; SUGARS 8g (est. added sugars 1g); CHOL 17mg; IRON 6mg; SODIUM 467mg; CALC 188mg

CHAPTER 5

10-MINUTE TREATS

With all due respect to professional pastry chefs, chocolate, sugar, ice cream, and cookies don't need too much help to taste delicious. In less time than it takes to decipher the difference between a tart and a torte, you can whip up a batch of Baklava Bites, Cashew Tarts, or Mango-Pineapple Foster. There's nothing sweeter than spending less time in the kitchen and more time at the table with the people—and desserts—you love.

BAKLAVA BITES ▶

Baklava has a bad reputation for being difficult to prepare, but these nutty, fragrant tartlets save tons of time by using frozen phyllo shells.

SERVES 15 • HANDS-ON TIME: 5 MIN. • TOTAL TIME: 10 MIN.

1   (1.9-ounce) package frozen mini phyllo shells, thawed
3   tablespoons honey
1   tablespoon butter, melted
¼   teaspoon ground cinnamon

¼   teaspoon grated orange rind
⅛   teaspoon salt
⅓   cup finely chopped toasted walnuts
¼   cup finely chopped toasted pistachios

1 Preheat oven to 425°F. Place phyllo shells on a baking sheet. Combine honey and next 4 ingredients (through salt) in a small bowl. Stir in nuts; divide mixture among phyllo shells.

2 Bake at 425°F for 5 minutes or until shells are lightly toasted.

SERVING SIZE: 1 baklava bite

CALORIES 63; FAT 3.8g (sat 0.8g, mono 0.9g, poly 1.5g); PROTEIN 1g; CARB 6g; FIBER 0g; SUGARS 4g (est. added sugars 3g); CHOL 2mg; IRON 0mg; SODIUM 39mg; CALC 6mg

ALMOND-DATE BARS

Marcona almonds are blanched and roasted—you won't need to toast them. For the best texture, use whole pitted dates for their stickiness.

SERVES 12 • HANDS-ON TIME: 10 MIN. • TOTAL TIME: 10 MIN.

1   cup Marcona almonds
1¼ cups pitted dates (about 15)
¾   cup dried apples (about 2 ounces)
¼   cup flaked sweetened coconut

1   tablespoon honey
⅛   teaspoon kosher salt
¾   cup crispy rice cereal
Cooking spray

1 Place first 6 ingredients in the bowl of a food processor; process until finely chopped. Add cereal; pulse to combine. Press date mixture into bottom of an 8-inch square glass or ceramic baking dish coated with cooking spray. Cut into 12 bars.

SERVING SIZE: 1 bar

CALORIES 142; FAT 6.3g (sat 1g, mono 3.7g, poly 1.5g); PROTEIN 3g; CARB 22g; FIBER 3g; SUGARS 17g (est. added sugars 1g); CHOL 0mg; IRON 1mg; SODIUM 76mg; CALC 36mg

BROILED PEACHES
WITH MASCARPONE

A little caramelization and cream puts the peach harvest to good use. Don't want to turn on the oven? A small culinary torch—the kind you'd use for crème brûlée—does the job just as well.

SERVES 4 • HANDS-ON TIME: 9 MIN. • TOTAL TIME: 9 MIN.

2   medium-sized ripe peaches, halved and pitted
3   tablespoons sugar, divided
2   tablespoons mascarpone cheese, softened (such as Vermont Creamery)
½   teaspoon vanilla bean paste
2   tablespoons whipping cream
2   tablespoons chopped, dry-roasted, salted pistachios

1 Preheat broiler. Arrange peach halves on a foil-lined baking sheet. Sprinkle each peach half with 2 teaspoons sugar. Broil 6 minutes or until sugar is golden and peaches are tender.

2 Combine remaining 1 teaspoon sugar, mascarpone cheese, and vanilla bean paste in a bowl, stirring with a whisk until smooth. Gradually add cream, beating with whisk until soft peaks form.

3 Place peach halves on each of 4 plates; top each with mascarpone mixture and pistachios.

SERVING SIZE: 1 peach, 1½ tablespoons marscapone mixture, and 1½ teaspoons pistachios
CALORIES 171; FAT 10.8g (sat 5.2g, mono 4.1g, poly 0.6g); PROTEIN 2g; CARB 18g; FIBER 1g; SUGARS 16g (est. added sugars 9g); CHOL 25mg; IRON 0mg; SODIUM 30mg; CALC 35mg

Savvy Shortcuts

If you're short on time, skip the mascarpone and whipping cream, and top the broiled peaches with a scoop of reduced-fat vanilla bean ice cream instead.

CARAMEL-GINGER ICE-CREAM SANDWICHES

Chopped pecans and ginger dress up the sides of these sweet and spicy treats. For firmer sandwiches, freeze up to two hours before serving.

SERVES 6 • HANDS-ON TIME: 5 MIN. • TOTAL TIME: 10 MIN.

⅓ cup finely chopped toasted pecans
1 tablespoon finely chopped crystallized ginger
1¼ cups caramel-swirl light ice cream (such as Edy's Slow Churned Caramel Delight)

12 thin gingersnap cookies (such as Anna's)

1 Combine pecans and crystallized ginger in a small bowl.

2 Scoop a scant ¼ cup ice cream onto flat side of each of 6 cookies. Top with remaining 6 cookies, flat sides down; press gently.

3 Roll edges of sandwiches in pecan mixture, pressing gently to adhere. Place sandwiches in a baking pan; freeze 5 minutes.

SERVING SIZE: 1 ice-cream sandwich

CALORIES 142; FAT 7.5g (sat 2.2g, mono 2.5g, poly 1.3g); PROTEIN 2g; CARB 17g; FIBER 1g; SUGARS 11g (est. added sugars 6g); CHOL 8mg; IRON 0mg; SODIUM 66mg; CALC 29mg

CHOCOLATE-FLECKED CANNOLI

Easily made ahead and refrigerated, these tasty little treats are a great way to end an Italian dinner. If you can't find candied orange peel, substitute ½ teaspoon orange rind instead.

SERVES 7 • HANDS-ON TIME: 10 MIN. • TOTAL TIME: 10 MIN.

¾ cup part-skim ricotta cheese, drained
2 ounces ⅓-less-fat cream cheese (about ¼ cup), softened
¼ cup powdered sugar
1 tablespoon sweet marsala wine
1 ounce bittersweet chocolate, chopped
1 tablespoon chopped candied orange peel
14 (3-inch-long) mini cannoli shells (such as Alessi)
2 tablespoons finely chopped salted, dry-roasted pistachios

1 Place first 4 ingredients in a food processor; process until smooth. Add chocolate and candied orange peel; pulse 4 to 5 times or until blended.

2 Place ricotta mixture in a small heavy-duty zip-top plastic bag; seal bag. Snip a ¾-inch hole in 1 bottom corner of bag. Fill cannoli shells evenly with ricotta mixture. Sprinkle pistachios onto ends of cannoli.

SERVING SIZE: 2 cannoli

CALORIES 196; FAT 9.7g (sat 3.3g, mono 2.1g, poly 0.9g); PROTEIN 7g; CARB 21g; FIBER 1g; SUGARS 10g (est. added sugars 5g); CHOL 24mg; IRON 1mg; SODIUM 65mg; CALC 87mg

Savvy Shortcuts

To drain ricotta, place in a sieve lined with several layers of paper towels, and let stand 20 minutes.

AFFOGATO
WITH MOCHA SAUCE

Italian for "drowned," affogato combines coffee, ice cream, and chocolate in a sophisticated dessert that comes together quickly but tastes like it took all day. Top each serving with chocolate curls, if you like.

SERVES 4 • HANDS-ON TIME: 9 MIN. • TOTAL TIME: 9 MIN.

¼ cup half-and-half
⅓ cup premium bittersweet chocolate chips
¼ cup powdered sugar
1 tablespoon light corn syrup

5 tablespoons Kahlúa (coffee-flavored liqueur), divided
1⅓ cups vanilla low-fat ice cream
¾ cup hot brewed espresso or strong coffee

1 Bring half-and-half to a simmer in a small saucepan over medium-low heat. Reduce heat to low, and add chocolate; cook, stirring constantly with a whisk, 1 minute or until smooth. Stir in powdered sugar, corn syrup, and 1 tablespoon liqueur; cook, stirring constantly with a whisk, 1 minute or until smooth.

2 Spoon ice cream into each of 4 glasses; top each serving with hot espresso, remaining liqueur, and mocha sauce. Serve immediately.

SERVING SIZE: ⅓ cup ice cream, 3 tablespoons hot espresso, 1 tablespoon liqueur, and 2 tablespoons mocha sauce

CALORIES 281; FAT 9.9g (sat 5.8g, mono 3g, poly 0.3g); PROTEIN 3g; CARB 41g; FIBER 1g; SUGARS 35g (est. added sugars 27g); CHOL 19mg; IRON 1mg; SODIUM 48mg; CALC 58mg

◀ MOCHA-PECAN SUNDAES

A healthier alternative to brownies, premade Belgian waffles make a great base for this fruity, fudgy sundae.

SERVES 4 • HANDS-ON TIME: 7 MIN. • TOTAL TIME: 7 MIN.

3   (1.3-ounce) frozen Belgian waffles (such as Van's)
1⅓ cups coffee low-fat ice cream

¼   cup fat-free fudge topping, warmed
1   cup sliced strawberries
¼   cup chopped toasted pecans

1 Toast waffles according to package directions. Cut each waffle diagonally into quarters; place pieces in each of 4 shallow bowls. Top each serving with ice cream, warmed hot fudge, strawberries, and pecans.

SERVING SIZE: 3 waffle pieces, ⅓ cup ice cream, 1 tablespoon hot fudge, ¼ cup strawberries, and 1 tablespoon pecans

CALORIES 274; FAT 11.1g (sat 2g, mono 4.5g, poly 2.3g); PROTEIN 5g; CARB 41g; FIBER 2g; SUGARS 20g (est. added sugars 12g); CHOL 13mg; IRON 1mg; SODIUM 114mg; CALC 79mg

APPLE PIE BITES

Forget the fork: These portable pies are filled with healthy fats instead of empty calories.

SERVES 10 • HANDS-ON TIME: 10 MIN. • TOTAL TIME: 10 MIN.

1¼ cups chopped dried apple rings
1   tablespoon fat-free caramel topping
2   pitted Medjool dates, chopped (¼ cup)

¼   cup chopped toasted pecans
1   tablespoon toasted wheat germ
1   teaspoon ground cinnamon
¼   teaspoon ground nutmeg

1 Place first 3 ingredients in a food processor; process 10 to 15 seconds or until mixture forms a paste, scraping sides of bowl as necessary.

2 Add pecans and remaining ingredients; pulse 6 to 8 times or until mixture is crumbly. With moist hands, roll mixture by tablespoonfuls into 10 balls.

SERVING SIZE: 1 ball

CALORIES 52; FAT 2.1g (sat 0.2g, mono 1.1g, poly 0.6g); PROTEIN 1g; CARB 9g; FIBER 1g; SUGARS 7g (est. added sugars 1g); CHOL 0mg; IRON 0mg; SODIUM 11mg; CALC 9mg

RICOTTA-HAZELNUT TOASTS

Propose a toast covered with nuts, creamy ricotta, and chocolate. Not a fan of seeded bread? Try a European-style crusty loaf instead.

SERVES 4 • HANDS-ON TIME: 10 MIN. • TOTAL TIME: 10 MIN.

2 (1¼-ounce) slices dense whole-wheat bread with seeds (such as Whole Foods Prairie Bread)
Cooking spray
2 tablespoons chopped blanched hazelnuts
2 tablespoons bittersweet chocolate chips
¼ cup part-skim ricotta cheese
1 tablespoon extra-virgin olive oil

1 Preheat oven to 375°F.

2 Coat bread slices with cooking spray. Place hazelnuts and bread slices on a foil-lined baking sheet. Bake at 375°F for 5 minutes or until bread is toasted. Remove bread from baking sheet. Bake hazelnuts an additional 3 minutes or until golden brown.

3 Place chocolate chips in a small microwave-safe bowl. Microwave at HIGH 30 seconds, stirring after 15 seconds.

4 Spread 2 tablespoons ricotta cheese on each bread slice; drizzle each with 1 tablespoon melted chocolate, and sprinkle with 1 tablespoon hazelnuts. Drizzle each with 1½ teaspoons olive oil. Cut toasts diagonally in half. Serve immediately.

SERVING SIZE: 1 toast triangle

CALORIES 181; FAT 12.6g (sat 2.9g, mono 8.1g, poly 1.1g); PROTEIN 5g; CARB 14g; FIBER 3g; SUGARS 2g (est. added sugars 1g); CHOL 5mg; IRON 1mg; SODIUM 92mg; CALC 55mg

ANGEL FOOD LEMON-BLUEBERRY TOAST

Just a few minutes in the oven turns a store-bought angel food cake into a warm, fluffy foundation for a fruity topping.

SERVES 6 • HANDS-ON TIME: 10 MIN. • TOTAL TIME: 10 MIN.

6 (1¼-ounce) angel food cake wedges
⅓ cup blueberry jam
2 tablespoons fresh lemon juice, divided
½ cup lemon low-fat yogurt (such as Wallaby Organic)

3 tablespoons ⅓-less-fat cream cheese, softened
1½ cups fresh blueberries

① Preheat oven to 375°F. Place cake wedges on a baking sheet. Bake at 375°F for 4 minutes or until lightly toasted.

② Combine blueberry jam and 1 tablespoon lemon juice in a small bowl, stirring until smooth. Combine yogurt, cream cheese, and remaining 1 tablespoon lemon juice in a medium bowl, stirring until smooth.

③ Place cake wedges on each of 6 plates. Top each wedge with cream cheese mixture, jam mixture, and blueberries.

SERVING SIZE: 1 slice cake, 1½ tablespoons cream cheese mixture, 2 teaspoons jam mixture, and ¼ cup blueberries
CALORIES 177; FAT 2g (sat 1.1g, mono 0.4g, poly 0.1g); PROTEIN 4g; CARB 38g; FIBER 1g; SUGARS 29g (est. added sugars 16g); CHOL 7mg; IRON 0mg; SODIUM 232mg; CALC 144mg

Seasonal Switch-Up

No fresh blueberries? No problem. Try cranberries or diced peeled pears and apples for the fall and winter months. Or pair with fig jam.

LEMON-COCONUT FIZZ

The islands feel a little closer after a glass of this refreshing drink. If you can't find lemongrass, use lemon zest instead.

SERVES 1 • HANDS-ON TIME: 7 MIN. • TOTAL TIME: 7 MIN.

Fast Freeze

When life hands you lemons, make lemonade. When life hands you leftover lemonade, pour it into ice-cube trays, freeze and use later as a yummy way to freshen up a glass of water.

¼ cup refrigerated fresh lemonade (such as Simply Lemonade)
¼ cup coconut milk (such as Silk Original Coconutmilk)
5 mint leaves
1 (2-inch) piece fresh lemongrass, peeled and chopped
1 (1-inch) lime rind strip
1 cup ice cubes, divided
¼ cup chilled club soda
Mint sprigs (optional)

1 Place first 5 ingredients in a cocktail shaker; muddle together using a muddler or wooden spoon, working mint, lemongrass, and lime rind together to release their oils. Add ½ cup ice cubes; cover shaker, and shake vigorously 20 seconds or until thoroughly chilled.

2 Place remaining ½ cup ice cubes in a tall glass; strain lemonade mixture into glass. Slowly add club soda; stir gently. Garnish with mint sprigs, if desired.

SERVING SIZE: ¾ cup

CALORIES 55; FAT 1.3g (sat 1.3g, mono 0g, poly 0g); PROTEIN 0g; CARB 10g; FIBER 0g; SUGARS 9g (est. added sugars 5g); CHOL 0mg; IRON 1mg; SODIUM 28mg; CALC 119mg

CHOCOLATE-BANANA QUESADILLAS

Quesadillas switch from savory to sweet in a snap. For an even more healthful treat, use whole-wheat tortillas.

SERVES 4 • HANDS-ON TIME: 7 MIN. • TOTAL TIME: 7 MIN.

2   (8-inch) fat-free flour tortillas
¼   cup chunky peanut butter
½   cup chopped ripe banana

2   tablespoons semisweet chocolate minichips
Cooking spray

① Spread 1 side of each tortilla with 2 tablespoons peanut butter, leaving a 1-inch border. Sprinkle banana and minichips evenly on bottom halves of tortillas; fold top halves over filling, and press gently to seal.

② Heat a large nonstick skillet over medium-high heat. Coat both sides of quesadillas with cooking spray. Add quesadillas to pan, placing straight sides together. Cook 1 minute on each side or until golden brown and chocolate melts.

③ Remove quesadillas from pan; cut each into 4 wedges.

SERVING SIZE: 2 wedges

CALORIES 197; **FAT** 10.4g (sat 2.2g, mono 4.7g, poly 2.5g); **PROTEIN** 6g; **CARB** 20g; **FIBER** 5g; **SUGARS** 7g (est. added sugars 2g); **CHOL** 0mg; **IRON** 1mg; **SODIUM** 169mg; **CALC** 60mg

BERRY MERINGUE MESS

You won't have to spend more than a few minutes trifling with this trifle inspired by the British dessert Eton Mess.

SERVES 4 • HANDS-ON TIME: 10 MIN. • TOTAL TIME: 15 MIN.

Fast Freeze

Don't just zest half that orange—citrus rind freezes beautifully. Just pop it in a freezer bag, and use it in pasta, cakes, salads, and fresh fish dishes all year long.

1   (10-ounce) package frozen mixed berries, thawed (2 cups)
1   tablespoon sugar
1   tablespoon Cointreau (orange-flavored liqueur)
⅓   cup light whipping cream
3   tablespoons vanilla fat-free yogurt
¼   teaspoon grated orange rind
12 commercial meringue cookies (such as Miss Meringue)

1 Combine first 3 ingredients in a small bowl. Let stand 5 minutes, stirring occasionally until sugar dissolves.

2 Place whipping cream, yogurt, and orange rind in a bowl; beat with a mixer at high speed 2 minutes or until stiff peaks form.

3 Break 6 cookies into pieces, and divide evenly among 4 small glasses or dessert dishes. Top with about 3 tablespoons berry mixture and about 2 tablespoons whipped cream mixture. Repeat procedure with remaining 6 cookies, remaining berry mixture, and remaining whipped cream mixture.

SERVING SIZE: 1 dessert

CALORIES 203; FAT 6.4g (sat 3.9g, mono 1.8g, poly 0.2g); PROTEIN 2g; CARB 36g; FIBER 2g; SUGARS 31g (est. added sugars 24g); CHOL 22mg; IRON 0mg; SODIUM 30mg; CALC 45mg

◀ CASHEW TARTS

With 5 ingredients and 10 minutes, you can create tasty one-bite treats.

SERVES 15 • HANDS-ON TIME: 10 MIN. • TOTAL TIME: 10 MIN.

½ cup marshmallow creme (such as Marshmallow Fluff)
¼ cup cashew butter
2 ounces ⅓-less-fat cream cheese

1 (1.9-ounce) package mini phyllo shells, thawed
15 bittersweet chocolate chips

1️⃣ Place first 3 ingredients in a bowl; beat with a mixer at medium-high speed until smooth.

2️⃣ Place cream cheese mixture in a heavy-duty zip-top plastic bag. Snip a small hole in 1 bottom corner of bag; pipe about 2 teaspoons mixture into each tart shell.

3️⃣ Place chocolate chips in a microwave-safe bowl. Microwave at HIGH 30 seconds or until melted and smooth, stirring after 15 seconds. Drizzle evenly over tops of tarts.

SERVING SIZE: 1 tart

CALORIES 66; FAT 3.8g (sat 1.1g, mono 1.6g, poly 0.4g); PROTEIN 2g; CARB 6g; FIBER 0g; SUGARS 3g (est. added sugars 2g); CHOL 3mg; IRON 0mg; SODIUM 45mg; CALC 7mg

CHOCOLATE-CHERRY BARK

Antioxidants make this a sweet-and-savory treat or 3 o'clock pick-me-up.

SERVES 12 • HANDS-ON TIME: 4 MIN. • TOTAL TIME: 19 MIN.

8 ounces dark chocolate, chopped (such as Ghirardelli 60% cacao)
¼ teaspoon grated orange rind

½ cup chopped unsalted pistachios
½ cup chopped dried tart cherries
¼ teaspoon sea salt flakes

1️⃣ Cover a baking sheet with parchment paper. Place chocolate and orange rind in a microwave-safe bowl. Microwave at HIGH 1 minute or until chocolate melts, stirring at 30-second intervals. Spread mixture into an 11½ x 9½-inch rectangle on parchment paper using an offset spatula. Sprinkle pistachios, cherries, and salt over chocolate.

2️⃣ Freeze 15 minutes or just until firm. Cut into 12 rectangles, and remove from parchment with a thin spatula.

SERVING SIZE: 1 (¾-ounce) rectangle

CALORIES 139; FAT 9.3g (sat 4.4g, mono 3.3g, poly 1g); PROTEIN 3g; CARB 16g; FIBER 4g; SUGARS 10g (est. added sugars 3g); CHOL 3mg; IRON 1mg; SODIUM 50mg; CALC 11mg

Eat Now & Later

Dress up a bowl of ice cream with a piece of chocolate bark.

CRISPY CEREAL TREATS

Dried fruit, pecans, and sunflower seeds elevate this childhood treat to adult dessert status. Make sure to have all your ingredients prepped before you melt the marshmallows; they cool very quickly and make stirring in the add-ins very difficult.

SERVES 20 • HANDS-ON TIME: 10 MIN. • TOTAL TIME: 15 MIN.

Cooking spray
2 tablespoons butter
1 (10-ounce) package miniature marshmallows
6 cups oven-toasted rice cereal (such as Rice Krispies)
½ cup chopped toasted pecans (about 2 ounces)

⅓ cup chopped dried apricots (about 1.5 ounces)
⅓ cup sweetened dried cranberries (about 1.5 ounces)
⅓ cup semisweet minichips
¼ cup toasted sunflower seed kernels (about 1 ounce)

1 Coat a 13 x 9-inch metal baking pan with cooking spray.

2 Melt butter in a Dutch oven over medium-low heat. Add marshmallows, and cook, stirring constantly, 2 minutes or until marshmallows melt. Working quickly, add cereal and remaining 5 ingredients, stirring until coated. Press cereal mixture into prepared pan.

3 Let stand 5 minutes. Cut into 20 bars.

SERVING SIZE: 1 bar

CALORIES 144; FAT 5.3g (sat 1.6g, mono 2g, poly 1.4g); PROTEIN 2g; CARB 25g; FIBER 1g; SUGARS 13g (est. added sugars 10g); CHOL 3mg; IRON 3mg; SODIUM 67mg; CALC 6mg

SKILLET PEACH COOKIE "CRUMBLE"

Toasted walnuts and gingersnap cookies add texture and crunch to this stovetop sweet. Mix it up with oatmeal or toffee cookies, if you like.

SERVES 4 • HANDS-ON TIME: 10 MIN. • TOTAL TIME: 10 MIN.

4   (1-ounce) gingersnaps, coarsely crumbled
3   tablespoons chopped walnuts
1   tablespoon butter
1   (20-ounce) package frozen sliced peaches, thawed and drained (3 cups)

3   tablespoons sugar
½   teaspoon ground cinnamon
⅓   cup peach nectar
1   teaspoon all-purpose flour
1   cup vanilla low-fat ice cream

1 Preheat oven to 375°F.

2 Place gingersnaps and walnuts on a rimmed baking sheet. Bake at 375°F for 6 to 8 minutes or until lightly toasted.

3 Melt butter in a large nonstick skillet over high heat. Add peaches; cook, uncovered, 2 minutes or until peaches begin to release juices, stirring occasionally. Sprinkle peaches with sugar and cinnamon; cook, uncovered, 3 to 4 minutes or until peaches are softened and syrupy, stirring occasionally. Combine peach nectar and flour in a small bowl, stirring with a whisk until smooth; stir into peach mixture. Bring to a simmer; cook, stirring constantly, 30 seconds or until thick.

4 Place peach mixture in each of 4 shallow bowls; sprinkle each serving with gingersnap mixture, and top each with ice cream.

Eat Now & Later

Cinnamon and walnuts mix nicely with pears or apples in the fall and winter months. Use fresh peaches in the summertime.

SERVING SIZE: ½ cup peach mixture, ⅓ cup gingersnap mixture, and ¼ cup ice cream

CALORIES 330; FAT 11g (sat 3.9g, mono 3.2g, poly 3.1g); PROTEIN 5g; CARB 57g; FIBER 3g; SUGARS 35g (est. added sugars 18g); CHOL 18mg; IRON 2mg; SODIUM 166mg; CALC 63mg

MANGO-PINEAPPLE FOSTER

Bananas Foster takes a trip to the tropics and makes a huge splash. Find precut mango and pineapple in the produce section of your supermarket. Double the recipe to feed a crowd.

SERVES 4 • HANDS-ON TIME: 8 MIN. • TOTAL TIME: 8 MIN.

2 tablespoons butter
⅓ cup packed light brown sugar
⅛ teaspoon freshly grated nutmeg
1 cup presliced mango, cut into ¼-inch-thick slices
1 cup (1-inch) cubed fresh pineapple

2 tablespoons dark rum
1 cup coconut- or lime-flavored low-fat sorbet
2 tablespoons chopped macadamia nuts
Freshly grated nutmeg (optional)

1 Melt butter in a large nonstick skillet over medium-high heat; stir in brown sugar and nutmeg. Cook 1½ minutes or until bubbly; stir in mango and pineapple. Cook, stirring constantly, 2 minutes or until fruit begins to release juices and sugar dissolves. Remove pan from heat. Pour rum into one side of pan. Ignite with a long match; let flames die down. Return pan to heat, and cook 1 minute or until sauce is smooth.

2 Place fruit mixture in each of 4 shallow bowls; top each serving with sorbet and macadamia nuts. Sprinkle with freshly grated nutmeg, if desired.

SERVING SIZE: ½ cup fruit mixture, ¼ cup sorbet, and 1½ teaspoons nuts

CALORIES 287; FAT 10.2g (sat 5.4g, mono 3.7g, poly 0.3g); PROTEIN 1g; CARB 47g; FIBER 2g; SUGARS 38g (est. added sugars 22g); CHOL 18mg; IRON 0mg; SODIUM 12mg; CALC 41mg

SUPER GREEN MACHINE

Kale is a superfood that doesn't always taste so super when raw. Masking it with pineapple, banana, and the bite of fresh ginger gives you all the benefits without the bitterness.

SERVES 2 • HANDS-ON TIME: 5 MIN. • TOTAL TIME: 5 MIN.

1 cup coconut water
1 cup (¾-inch) chunks fresh pineapple
1 tablespoon fresh lime juice
1 cup baby kale leaves (1½ ounces)

½ teaspoon grated peeled fresh ginger
½ cup ice cubes
1 (5-ounce) peeled banana, frozen and broken into 4 pieces

1 Place ingredients in the order given in a blender; process until smooth, scraping sides as necessary and adding additional ice until desired consistency.

SERVING SIZE: 1½ cups

CALORIES 131; **FAT** 0.5g (sat 0.1g, mono 0g, poly 0.1g); **PROTEIN** 2g; **CARB** 34g; **FIBER** 3g; **SUGARS** 20g (est. added sugars 0g); **CHOL** 0mg; **IRON** 1mg; **SODIUM** 40mg; **CALC** 53mg

SEXY ELVIS

Full of the King's favorites, this smoothie is packed with potassium and protein. Use powdered peanut butter for the same flavor and consistency as regular peanut butter without the calories.

SERVES 2 • HANDS-ON TIME: 5 MIN. • TOTAL TIME: 5 MIN.

Fast Freeze

Bananas brown quickly, so freeze ripe ones you can't use immediately for future smoothies. Just place them in a zip-top plastic bag in the freezer, and whip them out when you're ready to use.

½ cup dark chocolate-flavored almond milk
½ cup plain fat-free yogurt
2 tablespoons chocolate powdered peanut butter (such as PB2)

½ cup ice cubes
1 (5-ounce) peeled banana, frozen and broken into 4 pieces

1 Place all ingredients in the order given in a blender; pulse until banana and ice cubes are chopped. Process until smooth, scraping sides as necessary.

SERVING SIZE: 1 cup

CALORIES 136; **FAT** 1.4g (sat 0.1g, mono 0.7g, poly 0.3g); **PROTEIN** 6g; **CARB** 29g; **FIBER** 3g; **SUGARS** 18g (est. added sugars 2g); **CHOL** 1mg; **IRON** 1mg; **SODIUM** 129mg; **CALC** 196mg

CARROT CAKE SMOOTHIE

It's genius: Carrot cake in a cup curbs the craving for—and cuts the calories of—the original without all the flour and sugar.

SERVES 2 • HANDS-ON TIME: 5 MIN. • TOTAL TIME: 5 MIN.

⅔ cup bottled carrot juice (such as Bolthouse Farms)

½ cup vanilla low-fat frozen yogurt

¾ cup ice cubes

3 tablespoons unsalted creamy almond butter

¼ teaspoon ground cinnamon

¼ cup coarsely crushed gingersnap crumbs

1 Place all ingredients except cookies in a blender; process until smooth and creamy. Pour mixture into each of 2 glasses. Sprinkle each serving with 2 tablespoons cookie crumbs.

SERVING SIZE: ¾ cup and 2 tablespoons cookie crumbs

CALORIES 302; FAT 16.2g (sat 2.4g, mono 8.6g, poly 3.4g); PROTEIN 10g; CARB 31g; FIBER 3g; SUGARS 14g (est. added sugars 7g); CHOL 33mg; IRON 1mg; SODIUM 122mg; CALC 229mg

CHAPTER 6

EASY EXTRAS

The best meals are all about balance. We balance flavors, ingredients, and portions on the plate, but we also must balance our time, looking at each element of the meal and deciding what is and isn't deserving of it. When you purchase precooked meats and sides, you're not just buying food; you're buying time. Spend that extra time wisely on the aspects of a meal that make the most impact, like simple homemade sauces, salads, and dressings. Spinach is little more than leaves until you add Bacon Vinaigrette. Now that's a payoff worth the investment.

BACON VINAIGRETTE ▶

Lard have mercy, there's bacon in my dressing! This tasty twist on pig candy, also known as candied bacon, is the perfect way to punch up a spinach salad.

SERVES 4 • HANDS-ON TIME: 5 MIN. • TOTAL TIME: 8 MIN.

2   center-cut bacon slices
1½ tablespoons cider vinegar
1½ teaspoons brown sugar

1½ teaspoons Dijon mustard
⅛ teaspoon freshly ground black pepper
Dash of kosher salt

1 Cook bacon in a nonstick skillet over medium heat until crisp. Remove bacon from pan; crumble. Add vinegar, brown sugar, Dijon mustard, pepper, and salt to drippings in pan, stirring with a whisk. Stir in bacon.

SERVING SIZE: 2 tablespoons

CALORIES 20; FAT 0.7g (sat 0.25g, mono 0g, poly 0g); PROTEIN 1g; CARB 2g; FIBER 0g; SUGARS 2g (est. added sugars 2g); CHOL 3mg; IRON 0mg; SODIUM 119mg; CALC 2mg

CAESAR VINAIGRETTE ▶

Don't be fooled by those dramatic tableside presentations: Caesar dressing comes together fast. This lighter and lower-sodium version can also be used as a dip for crudités or a marinade for vegetables and chicken before roasting.

SERVES 4 • HANDS-ON TIME: 5 MIN. • TOTAL TIME: 5 MIN.

2   tablespoons grated fresh
    Parmesan cheese
1   tablespoon fresh lemon juice
½ teaspoon anchovy paste
¼ teaspoon freshly ground black pepper

¼ teaspoon Worcestershire sauce
1   large pasteurized egg yolk
1   garlic clove, minced
2   tablespoons extra-virgin olive oil

1 Place first 7 ingredients in a mini food processor; process 15 seconds. With processor on, gradually add oil, processing until combined.

SERVING SIZE: 2 tablespoons

CALORIES 88; FAT 8.7g (sat 1.8g, mono 5.6g, poly 0.9g); PROTEIN 2g; CARB 1g; FIBER 0g; SUGARS 0g (est. added sugars 0g); CHOL 51mg; IRON 0mg; SODIUM 83mg; CALC 36mg

CLOCKWISE FROM TOP: Grapefruit–Poppy Seed Vinaigrette
(page 268); Cilantro-Chile Vinaigrette (page 269);
Caesar Vinaigrette; Tomato Vinaigrette (page 269);
Bacon Vinaigrette; Herb Vinaigrette (page 268)

GRAPEFRUIT-POPPY SEED VINAIGRETTE

Full of fruit, texture, and tangy sweetness, this dressing does all the work in a simple salad. Just add some spinach, and serve.

SERVES 4 • HANDS-ON TIME: 5 MIN. • TOTAL TIME: 5 MIN.

3 tablespoons fresh grapefruit juice
4 teaspoons canola mayonnaise
2 teaspoons white wine vinegar
1 teaspoon honey
½ teaspoon grated grapefruit rind

2 tablespoons grapeseed oil
½ teaspoon poppy seeds
⅛ teaspoon kosher salt
⅛ teaspoon freshly ground black pepper

1 Combine first 5 ingredients in a bowl, stirring with a whisk. Gradually add oil, stirring constantly with a whisk. Stir in remaining ingredients. Refrigerate in an airtight container up to 5 days.

SERVING SIZE: 2 tablespoons

CALORIES 85; FAT 8.3g (sat 0.7g, mono 1.9g, poly 5.2g); PROTEIN 0g; CARB 3g; FIBER 0g; SUGARS 1g (est. added sugars 1g); CHOL 0mg; IRON 0mg; SODIUM 96mg; CALC 7mg

HERB VINAIGRETTE

This vinaigrette requires no effort, makes a lot, and keeps beautifully. Pour it over a spring mix or tossed arugula, or use it to dress up a pizza.

SERVES 13 • HANDS-ON TIME: 5 MIN. • TOTAL TIME: 5 MIN.

9 tablespoons white wine vinegar
1½ tablespoons wildflower honey
½ teaspoon fine sea salt

1 cup canola oil
3 tablespoons chopped fresh basil
3 tablespoons minced fresh chives

1 Combine first 3 ingredients in a medium bowl; slowly add oil, stirring with a whisk until combined. Stir in basil and chives. Refrigerate in an airtight container up to 5 days.

SERVING SIZE: 2 tablespoons

CALORIES 160; FAT 17.2g; (sat 1.3g, mono 10.9g, poly 4.9g); PROTEIN 0g; CARB 2g; FIBER 0g; SUGARS 2g (est. added sugars 2g); CHOL 0mg; IRON 0mg; SODIUM 86mg; CALC 2mg

TOMATO VINAIGRETTE

Even out of season, tomatoes can be the star of the salad. Highlight their essence in this dressing, which uses grape tomatoes grown year-round.

SERVES 4 • HANDS-ON TIME: 5 MIN. • TOTAL TIME: 5 MIN.

2 tablespoons minced fresh basil
2 tablespoons balsamic vinegar
1 tablespoon minced shallots
1 teaspoon Dijon mustard

10 grape tomatoes
1 garlic clove
2 tablespoons olive oil

1 Place first 6 ingredients in a mini food processor; process until smooth. Gradually add oil, processing until combined. Refrigerate in an airtight container up to 5 days.

SERVING SIZE: 2 tablespoons

CALORIES 73; FAT 6.8g (sat 0.9g, mono 4.9g, poly 0.7g); PROTEIN 0g; CARB 3g; FIBER 0g; SUGARS 2g (est. added sugars 0g); CHOL 0mg; IRON 0mg; SODIUM 33mg; CALC 8mg

CILANTRO-CHILE VINAIGRETTE

Flavors of the Far East and Southwest combine to create a sweet heat in this delicious dressing. Use it to make a taco slaw or as a marinade.

SERVES 4 • HANDS-ON TIME: 8 MIN. • TOTAL TIME: 8 MIN.

2 tablespoons olive oil
4 teaspoons fresh lime juice
1 tablespoon minced Fresno red chile
2 teaspoons fish sauce
1 teaspoon grated peeled fresh ginger

½ teaspoon sugar
1 garlic clove, mashed into a paste
1 tablespoon finely chopped fresh cilantro

1 Combine first 7 ingredients; stir with a whisk. Stir in cilantro. Refrigerate in an airtight container up to 5 days.

SERVING SIZE: 2 tablespoons

CALORIES 67; FAT 6.8g (sat 0.9g, mono 4.9g, poly 0.7g); PROTEIN 0g; CARB 2g; FIBER 0g; SUGARS 1g (est. added sugars 1g); CHOL 0mg; IRON 0mg; SODIUM 191mg; CALC 3mg

AVOCADO DRESSING

Available year-round and full of nutrients, avocados provide creaminess. Serve this on salad or with your next Mexican meal.

SERVES 6 • HANDS-ON TIME: 5 MIN. • TOTAL TIME: 5 MIN.

½ cup diced peeled ripe avocado
¼ cup cilantro leaves
1 tablespoon fresh lime juice

1 tablespoon olive oil
¼ teaspoon salt
¼ teaspoon hot sauce

1 Place all ingredients in a blender; process until smooth. Refrigerate in an airtight container up to 3 days.

SERVING SIZE: 2 tablespoons

CALORIES 41; FAT 4.1g (sat 0.6g, mono 2.9g, poly 0.5g); PROTEIN 0g; CARB 1g; FIBER 1g; SUGARS 0g (est. added sugars 0g); CHOL 0mg; IRON 0mg; SODIUM 105mg; CALC 2mg

AVOCADO-HERB DRESSING

Full of fresh herbs and a hint of heat, this dressing is also a cool upgrade to sour cream on a taco bar.

SERVES 20 • HANDS-ON TIME: 10 MIN. • TOTAL TIME: 10 MIN.

½ cup canola mayonnaise
¼ cup finely chopped green onions
¼ cup reduced-fat sour cream
1 tablespoon chopped fresh
   flat-leaf parsley
1 tablespoon chopped fresh chives
1 teaspoon chopped fresh tarragon

1 teaspoon anchovy paste
⅛ teaspoon salt
½ ripe peeled avocado
1 garlic clove, minced
2 tablespoons water
1 tablespoon white wine vinegar
3 drops hot sauce

1 Place first 10 ingredients in a food processor; process until smooth. With the processor on, add 2 tablespoons water, vinegar, and hot sauce through food chute, processing until blended. Refrigerate in an airtight container up to 3 days.

SERVING SIZE: 1 tablespoon

CALORIES 54; FAT 5.6g (sat 0.8g, mono 2.9g, poly 1.3g); PROTEIN 0g; CARB 1g; FIBER 0g; SUGARS 0g (est. added sugars 0g); CHOL 4mg; IRON 0mg; SODIUM 73mg; CALC 7mg

BUTTERMILK RANCH

There is nothing better than homemade ranch dressing. The combination of chives, parsley, and dill with the brightness of lemon and bite of garlic makes this recipe a dream for salads, French fries, and pretty much everything edible.

SERVES 4 • HANDS-ON TIME: 5 MIN. • TOTAL TIME: 5 MIN.

⅓ cup whole buttermilk

1 tablespoon canola mayonnaise

1 teaspoon fresh lemon juice

¼ teaspoon freshly ground black pepper

1 small garlic clove, grated

1½ teaspoons chopped fresh chives

¾ teaspoon minced fresh parsley

½ teaspoon minced fresh dill

1 Combine buttermilk and next 4 ingredients (through garlic), stirring with a whisk. Stir in remaining ingredients. Refrigerate in an airtight container up to 3 days.

SERVING SIZE: 1½ tablespoons

CALORIES 24; FAT 1.6g (sat 0.4g, mono 0.8g, poly 0.4g); PROTEIN 1g; CARB 1g; FIBER 0g; SUGARS 1g (est. added sugars 0g); CHOL 2mg; IRON 0mg; SODIUM 49mg; CALC 27mg

PEPPER-GARLIC SPICE RUB

This rub is complex in flavor yet simple in preparation. Use it to quickly season roasted or grilled beef and chicken.

SERVES 24 • HANDS-ON TIME: 5 MIN. • TOTAL TIME: 5 MIN.

2 tablespoons freshly ground black pepper

1 tablespoon Hungarian sweet paprika

1 tablespoon chili powder

1 tablespoon garlic powder

1 tablespoon dark brown sugar

2 teaspoons ground cumin

2 teaspoons chopped fresh sage

1½ teaspoons dry mustard

1 teaspoon ground coriander

1 teaspoon ground red pepper

1 Combine all ingredients in a small bowl. Store in an airtight container up to 1 month.

SERVING SIZE: 1 teaspoon

CALORIES 8; FAT 0.2g (sat 0g, mono 0g, poly 0.1g); PROTEIN 0g; CARB 2g; FIBER 1g; SUGARS 1g (est. added sugars 1g); CHOL 0mg; IRON 0mg; SODIUM 4mg; CALC 7mg

FROM LEFT: All-Purpose Rub;
Jerk Spice Rub; Pepper-Garlic
Spice Rub (page 271)

◀ JERK SPICE RUB

This traditional jerk seasoning packs a punch that is mellowed by the sweetness of sugar. You can further tame the heat by cutting back on the ground red pepper. Use this rub on pork, chicken, or fish.

SERVES 16 • HANDS-ON TIME: 5 MIN. • TOTAL TIME: 5 MIN.

1	tablespoon dried parsley	1	teaspoon grated fresh nutmeg
1	tablespoon dried onion flakes	1	teaspoon crushed red pepper
2	to 3 teaspoons ground red pepper	1	teaspoon ground allspice
2	teaspoons garlic powder	¼	teaspoon freshly ground black pepper
2	teaspoons ground thyme	¼	teaspoon ground star anise
2	teaspoons brown sugar	¼	teaspoon ground cinnamon
1½	teaspoons kosher salt		

1 Combine all ingredients in a small bowl. Store in an airtight container up to 1 month.

SERVING SIZE: about 1 tablespoon

CALORIES 5; FAT 0.1g (sat 0g, mono 0g, poly 0g); PROTEIN 0g; CARB 1g; FIBER 0g; SUGARS 1g (est. added sugars 1g); CHOL 0mg; IRON 0mg; SODIUM 118mg; CALC 5mg

◀ ALL-PURPOSE RUB

When guests ask for this recipe, just say it's an old family secret. Kick it up a few notches with freshly ground red pepper or chipotle powder.

SERVES 36 • HANDS-ON TIME: 5 MIN. • TOTAL TIME: 5 MIN.

3	tablespoons paprika	1	tablespoon freshly ground black pepper
2	tablespoons dried oregano		
2	tablespoons dried thyme	1	tablespoon chili powder
2	tablespoons kosher salt	2	teaspoons onion powder
1	tablespoon garlic powder		

1 Combine all ingredients in a small bowl. Store in an airtight container up to 6 months.

SERVING SIZE: 1 teaspoon

CALORIES 4; FAT 0.1g (sat 0g, mono 0g, poly 0g); PROTEIN 0g; CARB 1g; FIBER 0g; SUGARS 0g (est. added sugars 0g); CHOL 0mg; IRON 0mg; SODIUM 327mg; CALC 9mg

ROASTED GARLIC– BALSAMIC AIOLI

When garlic bathes in olive oil and bakes in the oven, it comes out soft, sweet, and with a slight nutty flavor. It's killer on a burger.

SERVES 4 • HANDS-ON TIME: 10 MIN. • TOTAL TIME: 65 MIN.

1 whole garlic head	1 teaspoon balsamic vinegar
1 teaspoon olive oil	Dash of kosher salt
2 tablespoons canola mayonnaise	

❶ Preheat oven to 375°F. Remove papery skin from garlic head (do not peel or separate cloves). Drizzle oil over garlic; wrap in foil. Bake at 375°F for 45 minutes. Cool 10 minutes.

❷ Separate cloves; squeeze to extract garlic pulp. Discard skins. Mash garlic. Stir in mayonnaise, vinegar, and salt. Refrigerate in an airtight container up to 3 days.

SERVING SIZE: 1 tablespoon

CALORIES 34; **FAT** 2.5g (sat 0.1g, mono 1.6g, poly 0.8g); **PROTEIN** 0g; **CARB** 2g; **FIBER** 0g; **SUGARS** 0g (est. added sugars 0g); **CHOL** 0mg; **IRON** 0mg; **SODIUM** 85mg; **CALC** 11mg

RED-PEPPER AIOLI

Building a better burger isn't always about toppings. Whip up this velvety spread with just five ingredients and a few minutes.

SERVES 16 • HANDS-ON TIME: 5 MIN. • TOTAL TIME: 5 MIN.

3 garlic cloves, peeled	¼ teaspoon crushed red pepper
½ cup canola mayonnaise	1 (7-ounce) bottle roasted red bell peppers, drained
½ teaspoon salt	

❶ Drop garlic through food chute with food processor on. Process until finely minced. Add remaining ingredients; process until well combined. Refrigerate in an airtight container up to 3 days.

SERVING SIZE: 1 tablespoon

CALORIES 23; **FAT** 2g (sat 0g, mono 1g, poly 0.8g); **PROTEIN** 0g; **CARB** 1g; **FIBER** 0g; **SUGARS** 0g (est. added sugars 0g); **CHOL** 0mg; **IRON** 0mg; **SODIUM** 157mg; **CALC** 1mg

SUN-DRIED TOMATO AIOLI

When it's cold outside and you long for a tomato off the vine, take comfort in this standout condiment that's perfect on lamb or portobello burgers.

SERVES 4 • HANDS-ON TIME: 17 MIN. • TOTAL TIME: 17 MIN.

10 sun-dried tomatoes, packed without oil
1 cup water
¼ cup canola mayonnaise
¼ teaspoon freshly ground black pepper
1 garlic clove, minced

1 Place sun-dried tomatoes and 1 cup water in a microwave-safe bowl; microwave at HIGH 2 minutes. Let stand 3 minutes. Drain. Place tomatoes, mayonnaise, pepper, and garlic in a mini food processor; pulse 10 times or until tomatoes are finely chopped. Refrigerate in an airtight container up to 3 days.

SERVING SIZE: 1 tablespoon

CALORIES 52; FAT 3.9g (sat 0g, mono 2.4g, poly 1.5g); PROTEIN 1g; CARB 3g; FIBER 1g; SUGARS 2g (est. added sugars 0g); CHOL 0mg; IRON 0mg; SODIUM 119mg; CALC 8mg

Fast Freeze

Don't trash those leftover sun-dried tomatoes! As long as they're not packed in oil, they'll save perfectly in a zip-top freezer bag—and you can enjoy the sunny taste of summer almost any time of the year.

SUN-DRIED TOMATO PESTO

Though tomatoes spend days drying out in the sun, they retain all their nutrients and give this pesto a deep color and intense flavor.

SERVES 8 • HANDS-ON TIME: 10 MIN. • TOTAL TIME: 10 MIN.

½ cup sun-dried tomatoes, packed without oil
¾ cup boiling water
1 cup chopped seeded plum tomato
½ cup basil leaves
2 tablespoons pine nuts
1 tablespoon olive oil
⅛ teaspoon freshly ground black pepper
4 garlic cloves

1 Combine sun-dried tomatoes and ¾ cup boiling water in a bowl; let stand 4 minutes. Drain and chop.

2 Place sun-dried tomatoes, plum tomato, and remaining ingredients in a blender; process 20 seconds or until a paste forms. Refrigerate in an airtight container up to 5 days.

SERVING SIZE: 2 tablespoons

CALORIES 44; FAT 3.4g (sat 0.4g, mono 1.7g, poly 1g); PROTEIN 1g; CARB 3g; FIBER 1g; SUGARS 2g (est. added sugars 0g); CHOL 0mg; IRON 1mg; SODIUM 10mg; CALC 13mg

PESTO MAYONNAISE

Flavored mayonnaise is the fastest way to wake up a ho-hum sandwich. Try this one on your favorite sub or in a pasta salad at your next picnic.

SERVES 4 • HANDS-ON TIME: 8 MIN. • TOTAL TIME: 8 MIN.

2 tablespoons canola mayonnaise
2 tablespoons Classic Pesto (page 277)
⅛ teaspoon salt
⅛ teaspoon freshly ground black pepper

1 Combine all ingredients in a bowl. Refrigerate in an airtight container up to 3 days.

SERVING SIZE: 1 tablespoon

CALORIES 57; FAT 5.3g (sat 1g, mono 1.4g, poly 0.5g); PROTEIN 1g; CARB 1g; FIBER 0g; SUGARS 0g (est. added sugars 0g); CHOL 4mg; IRON 0mg; SODIUM 188mg; CALC 48mg

CLASSIC PESTO

Pesto has a way of making everything taste fresh. Use it on pizza or pasta, polenta or mashed potatoes, or your favorite omelet.

SERVES 12 • HANDS-ON TIME: 8 MIN. • TOTAL TIME: 8 MIN.

2   tablespoons coarsely chopped walnuts or pine nuts
2   garlic cloves, peeled
3   tablespoons extra-virgin olive oil
4   cups basil leaves (about 4 ounces)
2   ounces grated fresh Parmesan cheese (about ½ cup)
¼   teaspoon salt

1 Drop nuts and garlic through food chute with food processor on; process until minced. Add oil; pulse 3 times. Add basil, cheese, and salt; process until finely minced, scraping sides of bowl once. Refrigerate in an airtight container up to 5 days.

SERVING SIZE: 1 tablespoon

CALORIES 64; FAT 5.7g (sat 1.3g, mono 2.8g, poly 1g); PROTEIN 3g; CARB 1g; FIBER 0g; SUGARS 0g (est. added sugars 0g); CHOL 3mg; IRON 0mg; SODIUM 134mg; CALC 95mg

Fast Freeze

This simple pesto tastes way better than store-bought and takes just a few minutes to make, so double or triple the recipe, and freeze batches for future use.

BARBECUE SAUCE

Spend a little extra time creating this sweet-and-spicy barbecue sauce from pantry staples and a few fresh veggies.

SERVES 12 • HANDS-ON TIME: 20 MIN. • TOTAL TIME: 20 MIN.

2   cups unsalted ketchup
¾   cup packed brown sugar
½   cup cider vinegar
¼   cup grated fresh onion (1 small)
2   tablespoons prepared mustard
2   tablespoons Worcestershire sauce
1   teaspoon kosher salt
½   teaspoon freshly ground black pepper
½   teaspoon crushed red pepper
½   teaspoon smoked paprika
2   garlic cloves, pressed

1 Combine all ingredients in a medium saucepan. Bring to a boil over medium-high heat, stirring occasionally. Reduce heat; simmer, uncovered, 10 minutes or until slightly thickened. Refrigerate in an airtight container up to 1 month.

SERVING SIZE: 2 tablespoons

CALORIES 57; FAT 0.1g (sat 0g, mono 0g, poly 0g); PROTEIN 0g; CARB 14g; FIBER 0g; SUGARS 12g (est. added sugars 8g); CHOL 0mg; IRON 0mg; SODIUM 117mg; CALC 10mg

FROM LEFT: Sriracha Ketchup;
Honey Mustard; Barbecue
Sauce (page 277)

◀ SRIRACHA KETCHUP

Two favorite condiments create one incredibly spicy sauce you'll want to slather on everything.

SERVES 11 • HANDS-ON TIME: 5 MIN. • TOTAL TIME: 5 MIN.

1 cup unsalted ketchup
¼ cup Sriracha (hot chile sauce, such as Huy Fong)

1 tablespoon lower-sodium soy sauce
1 tablespoon fresh lime juice

1 Combine all ingredients in a medium bowl. Refrigerate in an airtight container up to 1 month.

SERVING SIZE: 2 tablespoons

CALORIES 36; FAT 0g (sat 0g, mono 0g, poly 0g); PROTEIN 0g; CARB 9g; FIBER 0g; SUGARS 7g (est. added sugars 2g); CHOL 0mg; IRON 0mg; SODIUM 169mg; CALC 0mg

◀ HONEY MUSTARD

Homemade honey mustard tastes infinitely better than store-bought and has fewer preservatives and additives. Blend up a quick batch while chicken cooks.

SERVES 20 • HANDS-ON TIME: 5 MIN. • TOTAL TIME: 5 MIN.

½ cup canola mayonnaise
¼ cup Dijon mustard
¼ cup honey

2 tablespoons prepared mustard
¼ teaspoon freshly ground black pepper

1 Combine all ingredients in a small bowl. Refrigerate in an airtight container up to 1 month.

SERVING SIZE: 1 tablespoon

CALORIES 30; FAT 1.5g (sat 0g, mono 0.8g, poly 0.6g); PROTEIN 0g; CARB 4g; FIBER 0g; SUGARS 3g (est. added sugars 3g); CHOL 0mg; IRON 0mg; SODIUM 123mg; CALC 1mg

SALSA VERDE

Tomatillos grow in papery husks that come off easily and leave a sticky residue. Rinse them well before throwing them in the food processor.

SERVES 8 • HANDS-ON TIME: 5 MIN. • TOTAL TIME: 5 MIN.

8 tomatillos (about 12 ounces)
¼ cup chopped green onions
¼ cup chopped fresh cilantro
½ teaspoon salt
1 jalapeño pepper, seeded and quartered
1 (4.5-ounce) can chopped green chiles, undrained

1 Discard husks and stems from tomatillos. Place tomatillos and remaining ingredients in a food processor; pulse until coarsely chopped. Refrigerate in an airtight container up to 3 days.

SERVING SIZE: ¼ cup

CALORIES 16; FAT 0.4g (sat 0.1g, mono 0.1g, poly 0.2g); PROTEIN 1g; CARB 3g; FIBER 1g; SUGARS 2g (est. added sugars 0g); CHOL 0mg; IRON 0mg; SODIUM 334mg; CALC 7mg

MEDITERRANEAN SALSA

When the garden gives you too much of everything, turn it into salsa.

SERVES 6 • HANDS-ON TIME: 10 MIN. • TOTAL TIME: 10 MIN.

1½ cups chopped seeded tomato
1 cup finely chopped zucchini
½ cup finely chopped bottled roasted red bell peppers
2 tablespoons finely chopped red onion
1 tablespoon finely chopped basil
1 tablespoon finely chopped parsley
2 teaspoons fresh lemon juice
2 teaspoons extra-virgin olive oil
1½ teaspoons capers, drained
¼ teaspoon salt
⅛ teaspoon freshly ground black pepper
1 garlic clove, minced

1 Combine all ingredients in a bowl. Refrigerate in an airtight container up to 2 days.

SERVING SIZE: ½ cup

CALORIES 32; FAT 1.7g (sat 0.3g, mono 1.2g, poly 0.2g); PROTEIN 1g; CARB 4g; FIBER 1g; SUGARS 2g (est. added sugars 0g); CHOL 0mg; IRON 0mg; SODIUM 183mg; CALC 12mg

CUTTING-BOARD SALSA

Did someone say "salsa party"? This chunky number is loaded with crunch and cool, crisp flavors.

SERVES 14 • HANDS-ON TIME: 20 MIN. • TOTAL TIME: 60 MIN., INCLUDING CHILL TIME

2	cups diced tomato	2	tablespoons chopped fresh mint
½	cup diced peeled jicama	2	tablespoons chopped fresh cilantro
½	cup diced onion	2	tablespoons fresh lime juice
½	cup diced radishes	2	teaspoons chopped seeded
⅓	cup chopped seeded peeled cucumber		jalapeño pepper (1 small pepper)
¼	cup fresh orange juice	½	teaspoon salt

1 Combine all ingredients in a large bowl; toss gently. Cover and chill 40 minutes. Refrigerate in an airtight container up to 2 days.

SERVING SIZE: ¼ cup

CALORIES 13; FAT 0.1g (sat 0g, mono 0g, poly 0.1g); PROTEIN 0g; CARB 3g; FIBER 1g; SUGARS 2g (est. added sugars 0g); CHOL 0mg; IRON 0mg; SODIUM 88mg; CALC 7mg

MANGO SALSA

Mango is one of the few fruits that can stand up to jalapeño in both texture and taste. Serve with grilled meats or fish.

SERVES 6 • HANDS-ON TIME: 15 MIN. • TOTAL TIME: 45 MIN., INCLUDING CHILL TIME

3	cups cubed peeled ripe mango	3	tablespoons finely chopped seeded
1	cup chopped green onions		jalapeño pepper (about 2 peppers)
½	cup chopped fresh cilantro	1	teaspoon sugar
⅓	cup fresh lime juice	½	teaspoon salt

1 Combine all ingredients in a bowl; toss well. Cover and chill 30 minutes. Refrigerate in an airtight container up to 3 days.

SERVING SIZE: ½ cup

CALORIES 63; FAT 0.3g (sat 0.1g, mono 0.1g, poly 0.1g); PROTEIN 1g; CARB 18g; FIBER 2g; SUGARS 13g (est. added sugars 1g); CHOL 0mg; IRON 0mg; SODIUM 205mg; CALC 25mg;

Savvy Shortcuts

Mango isn't the easiest fruit to chop. Save the hassle if you're short on time and purchase prepeeled and prechopped mango from your grocer's produce department.

NUTRITIONAL INFORMATION

HOW TO USE IT AND WHY

To interpret the nutritional analysis in *Dinner A.S.A.P.*, use the figures below as a daily reference guide. One size doesn't fit all, so take lifestyle, age, and circumstances into consideration. For example, pregnant or breast-feeding women need more protein, calories, and calcium. Go to choosemyplate.gov for your own individualized plan.

IN OUR NUTRITIONAL ANALYSIS, WE USE THESE ABBREVIATIONS

sat	saturated fat	**carb**	carbohydrates	**g**	gram
mono	monounsaturated fat	**chol**	cholesterol	**mg**	milligram
poly	polyunsaturated fat	**calc**	calcium		

DAILY NUTRITION GUIDE

	Women ages 25 to 50	Women over 50	Men ages 25 to 50	Men over 50
Calories	2,000	2,000*	2,700	2,500
Protein	50 g	50 g	63 g	60 g
Fat	65 g*	65 g*	88 g*	83 g*
Saturated Fat	20 g*	20 g*	27 g*	25 g*
Carbohydrates	304 g	304 g	410 g	375 g
Fiber	25g to 35 g	25 g to 35 g	25 g to 35 g	25 g to 35 g
Cholesterol	300 mg*	300 mg*	300 mg*	300 mg*
Iron	18 mg	8 mg	8 mg	8 mg
Sodium	2,300 mg*	1,500 mg*	2,300 mg*	1,500 mg*
Calcium	1,000 mg	1,200 mg	1,000 mg	1,000 mg

*Or less, for optimum health

Nutritional values used in our calculations either come from The Food Processor, Version 10.4 (ESHA Research), or are provided by food manufacturers.

METRIC EQUIVALENTS

The information in the following charts is provided to help cooks outside the United States successfully use the recipes in this book. All equivalents are approximate.

COOKING/OVEN TEMPERATURES

	Fahrenheit	Celsius	Gas Mark
Freeze Water	32° F	0° C	
Room Temp.	68° F	20° C	
Boil Water	212° F	100° C	
Bake	325° F	160° C	3
	350° F	180° C	4
	375° F	190° C	5
	400° F	200° C	6
	425° F	220° C	7
	450° F	230° C	8
Broil		Grill	

LIQUID INGREDIENTS BY VOLUME

¼ tsp	=					1 ml	
½ tsp	=					2 ml	
1 tsp	=					5 ml	
3 tsp	=	1 Tbsp	=	½ fl oz	=	15 ml	
2 Tbsp	=	⅛ cup	=	1 fl oz	=	30 ml	
4 Tbsp	=	¼ cup	=	2 fl oz	=	60 ml	
5⅓ Tbsp	=	⅓ cup	=	3 fl oz	=	80 ml	
8 Tbsp	=	½ cup	=	4 fl oz	=	120 ml	
10⅔ Tbsp	=	⅔ cup	=	5 fl oz	=	160 ml	
12 Tbsp	=	¾ cup	=	6 fl oz	=	180 ml	
16 Tbsp	=	1 cup	=	8 fl oz	=	240 ml	
1 pt	=	2 cups	=	16 fl oz	=	480 ml	
1 qt	=	4 cups	=	32 fl oz	=	960 ml	
				33 fl oz	=	1000 ml	= 1 l

DRY INGREDIENTS BY WEIGHT

(To convert ounces to grams, multiply the number of ounces by 30.)

1 oz	=	¹⁄₁₆ lb	=	30 g
4 oz	=	¼ lb	=	120 g
8 oz	=	½ lb	=	240 g
12 oz	=	¾ lb	=	360 g
16 oz	=	1 lb	=	480 g

LENGTH

(To convert inches to centimeters, multiply inches by 2.5.)

1 in	=				2.5 cm	
12 in	=	1 ft		=	30 cm	
36 in	=	3 ft	= 1 yd	=	90 cm	
40 in	=				100 cm	= 1 m

EQUIVALENTS FOR DIFFERENT TYPES OF INGREDIENTS

Standard Cup	Fine Powder (ex. flour)	Grain (ex. rice)	Granular (ex. sugar)	Liquid Solids (ex. butter)	Liquid (ex. milk)
1	140 g	150 g	190 g	200 g	240 ml
¾	105 g	113 g	143 g	150 g	180 ml
⅔	93 g	100 g	125 g	133 g	160 ml
½	70 g	75 g	95 g	100 g	120 ml
⅓	47 g	50 g	63 g	67 g	80 ml
¼	35 g	38 g	48 g	50 g	60 ml
⅛	18 g	19 g	24 g	25 g	30 ml

INDEX

A

Apple Pie Bites, 243
Apricot Skewers, Spiced Chicken and, 92
Artichokes with Lemon Aioli,
    Roasted Baby, 182
Asparagus
    Chicken Roulade, Mediterranean, 84
    Roasted Asparagus with Pecorino and
        Pine Nuts, 178
    Salmon with Whole-Grain Pilaf, Grilled, 62
    Scallops with Asparagus and Peas in
        Lemon Sauce, Seared, 131
    Shaved Asparagus with Manchego and
        Almonds, 196
Avocados
    Dressing, Avocado, 270
    Dressing, Avocado-Herb, 270
    Salad, Simple Avocado, 223

B

Banana Quesadillas, Chocolate-, 251
Bananas, in Sexy Elvis, 262
Basil, Feta, and Tomatoes, Shaved Summer
    Squash with, 153
Basil, in Classic Pesto, 277
Beans and Legumes
    Lentils with Goat Cheese, Warm, 157
    Pilaf, Black Bean and Corn, 34
    Salad, Mediterranean Chickpea, 228
    Salad, Multibean, 191
    Tostadas with Cilantro Slaw, Chicken and
        Black Bean, 21
Beef
    Burritos, Picadillo, 42
    Flank Steak, Soy-Ginger, 108
    Hamburger Steak with Onion-Mushroom
        Gravy, 104
    Negimaki, Quick, 107
    Pho, Quick Beef, 45
    Salad, Steak, Pear, and Watercress, 216

Sandwiches, Roast Beef-Blue Cheese, 41
Shepherd's Pie, 46
Skirt Steak with Mojo, Cuban-Style, 103
Tacos with Salsa Verde, Shredded Beef, 49
Beet Carpaccio Salad, 211
Berry Meringue Mess, 252
Beverages
    Carrot Cake Smoothie, 263
    Lemon-Coconut Fizz, 248
    Sexy Elvis, 262
    Super Green Machine, 262
Blueberry Chicken Salad, Creamy, 199
Blueberry Toast, Angel Food Lemon-, 247
Bread, in Heirloom Tomato Panzanella, 203
Bread Salad, Pita, 30
Broccoli
    Charred Broccoli with Orange Browned
        Butter, 161
    Pasta Toss, Lemon-Broccoli, 22
    Salad, Crunchy Autumn, 215
    Slaw, Asian Broccoli, 54
Brussels Sprouts
    Roasted Brussels Sprouts with Ham
        and Garlic, 146
    Salad, Crunchy Autumn, 215
    Salad, Wheat Berry and Brussels
        Sprouts, 38
Butternut Broth, Mushroom Ravioli and
    Winter Vegetables in, 74

C

Caper Sauce, Lemon-, 66
Carrots
    Glazed Carrots, Honey-Ginger, 177
    Salad, Sesame-Carrot Edamame, 208
    Smoothie, Carrot Cake, 263
Cheese
    Macaroni and Cheese, Stovetop, 181
    Mashed Potatoes, Bacon and Cheddar, 162
    Peaches with Mascarpone, Broiled, 235
    Sandwiches, Roast Beef-Blue Cheese, 41
    Stuffed Chicken Breasts, Roasted
        Tomato-Cheese, 88
    Toasts, Ricotta-Hazelnut, 244
Cherry Bark, Chocolate-, 255

Chicken
    Andouille, Creole Shrimp with, 127
    Cutlets over Lemon-Broccoli Pasta Toss,
        Parmesan-Crusted Chicken, 22
    Cutlets with Rice Noodles, Thai Peanut
        Chicken, 33
    Fajitas, Chipotle-Spiked Chicken, 83
    Fried Rice with Edamame, Chicken, 80
    Kebabs with Pita Bread Salad, Chicken, 30
    Noodles with Snow Peas, Peanutty
        Chicken, 25
    Orzo, Mediterranean Chicken, 29
    Pasta, Chicken Meatball Angel Hair, 18
    Pepper Jelly-Glazed Chicken, 96
    Pizza, Tandoori Chicken, 95
    Roulade, Mediterranean Chicken, 84
    Salad, Creamy Blueberry Chicken, 199
    Skewers, Spiced Chicken and Apricot, 92
    Skillet Dinner, Weeknight Lemon
        Chicken, 87
    Soup with Chicken and Vegetables, Thai
        Curry-Lime, 26
    Stuffed Chicken Breasts, Roasted Tomato-
        Cheese, 88
    Tabbouleh with Chicken and Red
        Pepper, 192
    Tenders, Coconut-Crusted Chicken, 99
    Tostadas with Cilantro Slaw, Chicken and
        Black Bean, 21
    Wraps with Jicama-Pineapple Slaw,
        Chicken, 91
Chocolate
    Affogato with Mocha Sauce, 240
    Bark, Chocolate-Cherry, 255
    Quesadillas, Chocolate-Banana, 251
    Sexy Elvis, 262
    Sundaes, Mocha-Pecan, 243
Cilantro
    Slaw, Cilantro, 21
    Slaw, Cilantro-Avocado, 70
    Vinaigrette, Cilantro-Chile, 269
Citrus Salad, Roasted Fennel-, 219
Citrus Vinaigrette, 200
Coconut
    Chicken Tenders, Coconut-Crusted, 99
    Fizz, Lemon-Coconut, 248
    Soup, Thai Coconut Shrimp, 65

Coffee, in Affogato with Mocha Sauce, 240
Coffee, in Mocha-Pecan Sundaes, 243
Condiments
    Aiolis
        Lemon Aioli, 182
        Red-Pepper Aioli, 274
        Roasted Garlic-Balsamic Aioli, 274
        Sun-Dried Tomato Aioli, 275
    Hummus Grilled Veggie Wrap, Spicy-, 143
    Ketchup, Sriracha, 279
    Mayonnaise, Pesto, 276
    Mustard, Honey, 279
    Pesto, Classic, 277
    Pesto, Sun-Dried Tomato, 276
    Rubs
        All-Purpose Rub, 273
        Jerk Spice Rub, 273
        Pepper-Garlic Spice Rub, 271
    Salsas
        Cutting-Board Salsa, 281
        Mango Salsa, 116, 281
        Mediterranean Salsa, 280
        Salsa Verde, 280
Corn
    Grilled Corn with Chipotle-Lime Butter, 166
    Pilaf, Black Bean and Corn, 34
    Polenta, Tomatoes, Mushrooms, and
        Zucchini over Creamy Pesto, 140
Cucumber-Mint Raita, 207

D

Date Bars, Almond, 232
Desserts
    Affogato with Mocha Sauce, 240
    Baklava Bites, 232
    Bark, Chocolate-Cherry, 255
    Bars, Almond-Date, 232
    Cannoli, Chocolate-Flecked, 239
    Cereal Treats, Crispy, 256
    "Crumble," Skillet Peach Cookie, 259
    Foster, Mango-Pineapple, 260
    Ice-Cream Sandwiches, Caramel-
        Ginger, 236
    Mess, Berry Meringue, 252
    Peaches with Mascarpone, Broiled, 235

Pie Bites, Apple, 243
    Quesadillas, Chocolate-Banana, 251
    Sundaes, Mocha-Pecan, 243
    Tarts, Cashew, 255
    Toast, Angel Food Lemon-Blueberry, 247
    Toasts, Ricotta Hazelnut, 244
Dill Sauce, Lemon-, 170
Dressings and Salad Dressings. *See also*
    Vinaigrettes
        Avocado Dressing, 270
        Avocado-Herb Dressing, 270
        Buttermilk Ranch, 271
        Pomegranate-Orange Dressing, 188
        Raita, Cucumber-Mint, 207

E

Edamame, Chicken Fried Rice with, 80
Edamame Salad, Sesame-Carrot, 208
Eggs
    Caesar Vinaigrette, 266
    Shakshuka over Garlic Greens, Spicy, 139
    Shaved Asparagus with Manchego and
        Almonds, 196

F

Fennel-Citrus Salad, Roasted, 219
Figs with Sorghum-Balsamic Glaze, Pork
    Tenderloin and, 119
Fish and Shellfish
    Crab and Heirloom Tomato Salad, 220
    Salmon
        Grilled Salmon with Whole-Grain
            Pilaf, 62
        Salad, Smoked Salmon and Wheat
            Berry, 224
        Seared Salmon with Hoisin Glaze, 128
        Seared Salmon with Roasted Grape
            Tomatoes, 69
    Scallops with Asparagus and Peas in
        Lemon Sauce, Seared, 131
    Shrimp
        "Ceviche," Shrimp, 132
        Creole Shrimp with Andouille, 127

Kebabs with Charred Tomato
            Vinaigrette and Feta, Grilled
            Shrimp, 136
        Sauté with Jasmine Rice, Red Curry
            Shrimp, 73
        Soup, Thai Coconut Shrimp, 65
    Snapper with Olive-Bar Pan Sauce,
        Seared, 135
    Tilapia with Lemon-Caper Sauce, Almond-
        Crusted, 66
    White fish, in Fish Tacos with Cilantro-
        Avocado Slaw, 70
Freezing Tips
    bananas, 262
    broth, beef, 46
    citrus zest, 252
    juice cubes, 38
    lemonade cubes, 248
    lemongrass, 120
    mint, 173
    pesto, 277
    soup, 37
    tomatoes, sun-dried, 275
Fruited Couscous with Almonds, 185

G

Ginger
    Carrots, Honey-Ginger Glazed, 177
    Flank Steak, Soy-Ginger, 108
    Ice-Cream Sandwiches, Caramel-
        Ginger, 236
    Super Green Machine, 262
Grains. *See also specific grains*
    Pilaf, Grilled Salmon with Whole-Grain, 62
    Pilaf, Turkey Burgers with Black Bean
        and Corn, 34
    Grapefruit-Poppy Seed Vinaigrette, 268
Green Beans. *See Haricots Verts*
Greens. *See also specific greens*
    Asian Greens, Stir-Fried Pork and, 58
    Shakshuka over Garlic Greens, Spicy, 139
    Super Green Machine, 262

H

Haricots Verts, and Olive Salad, Roasted Tomato, 227
Haricots Verts with Warm Shallot Vinaigrette and Bacon, 169
Herbs
    Dressing, Avocado-Herb, 270
    Herbed Lamb Chops with Lemony Orzo Salad, 50
    Pork Tenderloin with Onions, Herb-Crusted, 111
    Sauce, Herb-Mushroom, 100
    Vinaigrette, Herb, 268
Honey-Ginger Glazed Carrots, 177
Honey Mustard, 279

J

Jicama-Pineapple Slaw, 91

K

Kale, in Crunchy Autumn Salad, 215

L

Lamb
    Chops with Lemony Orzo Salad, Herbed Lamb, 50
    Leg of Lamb, Grilled Boneless, 124
    Sliders with Feta and Minted Yogurt Sauce, Lamb, 123
Leftovers
    asparagus, roasted, 178
    bark, chocolate, 255
    beef
        hamburger patties, 104
        shredded, 49
        steak, 83, 108
    beer, 83
    chicken, chopped, 99
    chicken roulade, 84
    grilled sandwich, 41

jicama, 91
juice, 38
meatball sandwich, 18
pizza dough, 57
pork
    fried rice, 53
    with mango chutney, 115
    tenderloin, 111
potatoes, mashed, 162
salad
    Asian slaw, 165
    quinoa, 207, 212
    roasted tomato, 227
    smoked salmon, 224
    soba noodle, 200
soup, butternut squash, 74
summer rolls, 54
tilapia, 66
tomato vinaigrette, charred, 136
turkey, 100
vegetables, roasted, 149
Lemongrass Pork Skewers, 120
Lemons
    Aioli, Lemon, 182
    Chicken Skillet Dinner, Weeknight Lemon, 87
    Fizz, Lemon-Coconut, 248
    Orzo Salad, Lemony, 50
    Pasta Toss, Lemon-Broccoli, 22
    Sauces
        Lemon-Caper Sauce, 66
        Lemon-Dill Sauce, 170
        Lemon Sauce, 131
    Toast, Angel Food Lemon-Blueberry, 247
Lime Butter, Chipotle-, 166
Lime Soup with Chicken and Vegetables, Thai Curry-, 26

M

Mangos
    Foster, Mango-Pineapple, 260
    Salsa, Mango, 116, 281
    Sauce, Spicy Mango, 115
Marshmallow, in Crispy Cereal Treats, 256

Minted Yogurt Sauce, 123
Mint Raita, Cucumber-, 207
Mushrooms
    Fried Brown Rice with Mushroom and Pine Nut, 150
    Gravy, Onion-Mushroom, 104
    Ravioli and Winter Vegetables in Butternut Broth, Mushroom, 74
    Sauce, Herb-Mushroom, 100
    Soup, Turkey, Mushroom, and Wild Rice, 37
    Tomatoes, Mushrooms, and Zucchini over Creamy Pesto Polenta, 140

N

Nuts
    Baklava Bites, 232
    Bars, Almond-Date, 232
    Couscous with Almonds, Fruited, 185
    Fried Rice
        Mushroom and Pine Nut, Fried Brown Rice with, 150
        Red Pepper and Almonds, Fried Brown Rice with, 150
        Zucchini and Walnut, Fried Brown Rice with, 150
    Quinoa, Nutty Almond-Sesame Red, 158
    Salad, Candied Walnut, Pear, and Leafy Green, 204
    Tarts, Cashew, 255
    Toasts, Ricotta Hazelnut, 244

O

Olive-Bar Pan Sauce, 135
Olive Salad, Roasted Tomato, Haricots Verts, and, 227
Onion-Mushroom Gravy, 104
Onions, Herb-Crusted Pork Tenderloin with, 111
Oranges
    Browned Butter, Charred Broccoli with Orange, 161
    Dressing, Pomegranate-Orange, 188
    Mojo, 103
    Salad, Roasted Fennel-Citrus, 219

P

Pasta and Noodles

Angel Hair Pasta, Chicken Meatball, 18

Chicken Noodles with Snow Peas, Peanutty, 25

Couscous Salad Cups, 188

Couscous with Almonds, Fruited, 185

Lemon-Broccoli Pasta Toss, 22

Macaroni and Cheese, Stovetop, 181

Orzo, Mediterranean Chicken, 29

Orzo Salad, Lemony, 50

Pho, Quick Beef, 45

Ravioli and Winter Vegetables in Butternut Broth, Mushroom, 74

Rice Noodles, Thai Peanut Chicken Cutlets with, 33

Soba Noodle Salad with Citrus Vinaigrette, 200

Peach Cookie "Crumble," Skillet, 259

Peaches with Mascarpone, Broiled, 235

Pear, and Leafy Green Salad, Candied Walnut, 204

Pear, and Watercress Salad, Steak, 216

Peas

Noodles with Snow Peas, Peanutty Chicken, 25

Scallops with Asparagus and Peas in Lemon Sauce, Seared, 131

Sugar Snap Peas with Quick-Pickled Radishes, 173

Peppers

Aioli, Red-Pepper, 274

Fried Brown Rice with Red Pepper and Almonds, 150

Pizza, Smoked Pork and Pepper, 57

Shakshuka over Garlic Greens, Spicy, 139

Tabbouleh with Chicken and Red Pepper, 192

Vinaigrette, Cilantro-Chile, 269

Pineapple

Foster, Mango-Pineapple, 260

Slaw, Jicama-Pineapple, 91

Stir-Fried Pork and Asian Greens, 58

Pomegranate-Orange Dressing, 188

Poppy Seed Vinaigrette, Grapefruit-, 268

Pork

Bacon

Haricots Verts with Warm Shallot Vinaigrette and Bacon, 169

Mashed Potatoes, Bacon and Cheddar, 162

Vinaigrette, Bacon, 266

Banh Mi Tartine, Pork, 112

Fried Rice, Pork, 53

Ham and Garlic, Roasted Brussels Sprouts with, 146

Medallions with Mango Salsa, Jerk Pork, 116

Pulled Pork Summer Rolls with Asian Broccoli Slaw, 54

Skewers, Lemongrass Pork, 120

Smoked Pork and Pepper Pizza, 57

Stir-Fried Pork and Asian Greens, 58

Tenderloin

Herb-Crusted Pork Tenderloin with Onions, 111

Pork Tenderloin and Figs with Sorghum-Balsamic Glaze, 119

Roasted Pork Tenderloin with Spicy Mango Sauce, 115

Teriyaki Pork Tenderloin Mu Shu Wraps, 61

Potatoes, Bacon and Cheddar Mashed, 162

Potatoes, in Shepherd's Pie, 46

Q

Quinoa

Almond-Sesame Red Quinoa, Nutty, 158

Salad, Brown Rice and Quinoa Tex-Mex, 212

Salad with Cucumber-Mint Raita, Curried Quinoa, 207

R

Radishes, Quick-Pickled, 173

Rice

Cereal Treats, Crispy, 256

Fried Rice

Chicken Fried Rice with Edamame, 80

Mushroom and Pine Nut, Fried Brown Rice with, 150

Pork Fried Rice, 53

Red Pepper and Almonds, Fried Brown Rice with, 150

Zucchini and Walnut, Fried Brown Rice with, 150

Jasmine Rice, 73

Salad, Brown Rice and Quinoa Tex-Mex, 212

Soup, Turkey, Mushroom, and Wild Rice, 37

S

Salads

Autumn Salad, Crunchy, 215

Avocado Salad, Simple, 223

Beet Carpaccio Salad, 211

Blueberry Chicken Salad, Creamy, 199

Brown Rice and Quinoa Tex-Mex Salad, 212

Candied Walnut, Pear, and Leafy Green Salad, 204

Chickpea Salad, Mediterranean, 228

Couscous Salad Cups, 188

Crab and Heirloom Tomato Salad, 220

Fennel-Citrus Salad, Roasted, 219

Multibean Salad, 191

Orzo Salad, Lemony, 50

Panzanella, Heirloom Tomato, 203

Pita Bread Salad, 30

Quinoa Salad with Cucumber-Mint Raita, Curried, 207

Salmon and Wheat Berry Salad, Smoked, 224

Sesame-Carrot Edamame Salad, 208

Slaws

Asian Slaw, Crunchy, 165

Asian Broccoli Slaw, 54

Cilantro-Avocado Slaw, 70

Cilantro Slaw, 21

Jicama-Pineapple Slaw, 91

in Teriyaki Pork Tenderloin Mu Shu Wraps, 61

Soba Noodle Salad with Citrus Vinaigrette, 200

Spinach Salad with Pepper Jelly Vinaigrette, 195

Steak, Pear, and Watercress Salad, 216

Summer Squash with Basil, Feta, and Tomatoes, Shaved, 153

Tabbouleh with Chicken and Red Pepper, 192

Tomato, Haricots Verts, and Olive Salad, Roasted, 227

Wheat Berry and Brussels Sprouts Salad, 38

Sandwiches. *See also* Wraps

Lamb Sliders with Feta and Minted Yogurt Sauce, 123

Meatless "Chicken" Tinga Gyros, 77

Pork Banh Mi Tartine, 112

Roast Beef–Blue Cheese Sandwiches, 41

Sauces

Barbecue Sauce, 277

Herb-Mushroom Sauce, 100

Lemon

Lemon-Caper Sauce, 66

Lemon-Dill Sauce, 170

Lemon Sauce, 131

Mango Sauce, Spicy, 115

Minted Yogurt Sauce, 123

Mocha Sauce, 240

Mojo, 103

Olive-Bar Pan Sauce, 135

Onion-Mushroom Gravy, 104

Shopping Tips, 17, 79, 115, 135

Smoothies. *See also* Beverages

Sorghum-Balsamic Glaze, 119

Soups

Beef Pho, Quick, 45

Curry-Lime Soup with Chicken and Vegetables, Thai, 26

Shrimp Soup, Thai Coconut, 65

Soybeans, Green. *See* Edamame

Spinach

Gnocchi with Spinach and Pine Nuts, Browned-Butter, 174

Salad with Pepper Jelly Vinaigrette, Spinach, 195

Sesame-Garlic Spinach, Spicy, 154

Squash, Summer

Cakes with Lemon-Dill Sauce, Zucchini, 170

Fried Brown Rice with Zucchini and Walnut, 150

Shaved Summer Squash with Basil, Feta, and Tomatoes, 153

Tomatoes, Mushrooms, and Zucchini over Creamy Pesto Polenta, 140

Squash, Winter. *See* Butternut

T

Tomatillos, in Salsa Verde, 280

Tomatoes

Aioli, Sun-Dried Tomato, 275

Pesto, Sun-Dried Tomato, 276

Roasted Grape Tomatoes, 69

Roasted Tomato-Cheese Stuffed Chicken Breasts, 88

Salads

Crab and Heirloom Tomato Salad, 220

Panzanella, Heirloom Tomato, 203

Roasted Tomato, Haricots Verts, and Olive Salad, 227

Salsa, Cutting-Board, 281

Salsa, Mediterranean, 280

Shaved Summer Squash with Basil, Feta, and Tomatoes, 153

Tomatoes, Mushrooms, and Zucchini over Creamy Pesto Polenta, 140

Vinaigrette, Charred Tomato, 136

Vinaigrette, Tomato, 269

Tools and Equipment

culinary torch, 235

food processor, 112

mandoline, 112, 211

vegetable peeler, 153

Turkey

Andouille, Creole Shrimp with, 127

Burgers with Black Bean and Corn Pilaf, Turkey, 34

Roasted Turkey Tenderloins with Herb-Mushroom Sauce, 100

Roasted Turkey with Wheat Berry and Brussels Sprouts Salad, 38

Soup, Turkey, Mushroom, and Wild Rice, 37

V

Vegetables

Spring Vegetables, Roasted Baby, 149

Veggie Wrap, Spicy-Hummus Grilled, 143

Winter Vegetables in Butternut Broth, Mushroom Ravioli and, 74

Vinaigrettes

Bacon Vinaigrette, 266

Caesar Vinaigrette, 266

Cilantro-Chile Vinaigrette, 269

Citrus Vinaigrette, 200

Grapefruit-Poppy Seed Vinaigrette, 268

Herb Vinaigrette, 268

Pepper Jelly Vinaigrette, 195

Shallot Vinaigrette, Warm, 169

Tomato Vinaigrette, 269

Tomato Vinaigrette, Charred, 136

W

Watercress Salad, Steak, Pear, and, 216

Wheat Berry and Brussels Sprouts Salad, 38

Wheat Berry Salad, Smoked Salmon and, 224

Wraps

Burritos, Picadillo, 42

Chicken Wraps with Jicama-Pineapple Slaw, 91

Hummus Grilled Veggie Wrap, Spicy-, 143

Mu Shu Wraps, Teriyaki Pork Tenderloin, 61

Summer Rolls with Asian Broccoli Slaw, Pulled Pork, 54

Y

Yogurt Sauce, Minted, 123

Z

Zucchini. *See* Squash, Summer